Eccentric
PREACHERS

"I never knew a good horse which had not some odd habit or other, and I never yet saw a minister worth his salt who had not some quirk or oddity."
– *Charles Spurgeon, "John Ploughman's Talk" (1869)*

Eccentric PREACHERS

*Spiritual Lessons and Insights
from God's Peculiar People*

C. H. Spurgeon

UPDATED AND ANNOTATED
BY RON METHENY

ANEKO
PRESS

We enjoy hearing from our readers. Please contact us at www.anekopress.com/questions-comments with any questions, comments, or suggestions.

Cover Designer: Jonathan Lewis
Editors: Ron Metheny, R. Clark

Aneko Press

www.anekopress.com

Aneko Press, Life Sentence Publishing, and our logos are trademarks of
Life Sentence Publishing, Inc.
203 E. Birch Street
P.O. Box 652
Abbotsford, WI 54405

RELIGION / Christian Ministry / Preaching

Paperback ISBN: 979-8-88936-336-1
eBook ISBN: 979-8-88936-337-8

10 9 8 7 6 5 4 3 2 1

Available where books are sold

Contents

Principles of the Revised Text ix

Foreword xi

Spurgeon's Preface xv

Ch. 1: What Is Eccentricity? 1

Ch. 2: Who Has Been Called Eccentric? 21

Ch. 3: Causes of Eccentricity 43

Ch. 4: Hugh Latimer 65

Ch. 5: Hugh Peters 69

Ch. 6: Daniel Burgess 73

Ch. 7: John Berridge 77

Ch. 8: Rowland Hill 83

Ch. 9: Matthew Wilks 89

Ch. 10: William Dawson 95

Ch. 11: Jacob Gruber 101

Ch. 12: Edward Taylor..117

Ch. 13: Edward Brooke 125

Ch. 14: Billy Bray, the Uneducated Soul Winner............................135

In Conclusion..145

Acknowledgements 149

Select Bibliography 151

Additional Notes...155

Glossary of "Eccentric Preachers" and Other Notables 173

Similar Titles..191

Principles of the Revised Text

1. The basis of this revision is the definitive text of *Eccentric Preachers* as written by Charles Spurgeon, and published in 1879.

2. Of foremost consideration has been a style of simple conversational (modern-American) English that maintains faithfulness to the design, meaning, doctrine, and purpose of the "Prince of Preachers," Charles Spurgeon, who lived, preached, and wrote during the Victorian era in England.

3. The majority of linguistic archaisms have been modified to produce a more contemporary style of expression, while other select antiquated modes of vocabulary, sentence structure, punctuation, etc. have been retained, since these have gained a particular timeless quality and quaintness about them that are seemingly intrinsic to *Eccentric Preachers*.

4. The English Standard Version is the preferred Scripture translation used in this revision, yet a select variety of passages (as quoted by Spurgeon) from the Authorized (King James) Version have been retained – the older of the two translations being preferred in such cases to maintain textual integrity. All Scripture quotations have further been cited with references parenthetically in text.

5. Clarifying comments on the revised text have also been included as additional notes bracketed in text and as the body of Appendix A. A number of these comments serve to act as source notes for literary quotations that Spurgeon failed to acknowledge fully in his original text, while others serve to briefly explain allusions made to historic events, locations, figures, etc., or to offer a gloss meaning to obscure phrases used by Spurgeon in *Eccentric Preachers*.

6. The first names of historic personages, whom Spurgeon mentioned only by surname in his original text, have been added (in text) in this revision. A "Glossary of 'Eccentric Preachers' and Other Notables" is also provided among its back matter as the body of Appendix B.

7. Certain liberties have been taken by the editor in his citations of Spurgeon's originally quoted sources. The APA style – although slightly modified due to the unique nature of the work in hand – is the preferred mode used per this revision. Furthermore, the earliest known sources still existing and discoverable online by the editor are cited in conjunction with Spurgeon's blocked quotations; this, in at least a few known instances, has created anachronisms of sorts, and are obviously not the original editions of these sources used by Spurgeon in his writing *Eccentric Preachers* (c. 1879). Noted citations in the updated edition are given solely for the benefit of the twenty-first-century reader as they may, or may not, pertain to his or her desire for further study.

8. Finally, in regards to these principles of the updated edition's revised text (as listed above), this editor welcomes suggestions and constructive criticism.

   – Ron Metheny

Foreword

History and experience have both proved that the man who has truly been called of God to preach the gospel of Jesus Christ, and carries out his task with faithfulness, is often considered to be a strange and enigmatic man. One might even call him eccentric. To be true to the nature of the call, the preacher steps outside of the mainstream thinking of the world. His viewpoints are much different than what is to be found in the morning paper, the nightly news, or the lectures that are given at the public university. He is a man convicted by conscience, and the streams of his mind flow from the deep rivers of the revealed truth of God's Word. His particular dogmas and forthright way of speaking often label him a contrarian who goes against the grain, and in large measure, this is true; but oh, how thankful the world should be for this rare and special breed of men.

Because the man of God is in such a unique position, he comes to find that he is loved and hated for the exact same reason. He has one message to proclaim: Jesus Christ and Him crucified! Some people come to love him for it, and others are determined to hate him. He handles precious things, and by God's grace, some who cross his path really do see the precious gospel jewel that he displays. As a consequence, they come to love the strange and beautiful feet that brought them the message of God's salvation. Others are not of the same opinion. Some hear the same beautiful message and look at the precious jewel displayed before their eyes, but they do not see it as such. They have no appreciation for the gospel diamond or the man of God who holds it. Their hearts are bent towards despicable things, and so they conclude that the preacher is mad. The man of God stands before men pleading over their souls, exhorting them to seek a saving interest in Christ. One onlooker says, "Oh, I feel sorry for the poor fellow all troubled again over such silly things." Another listens and beholds this strange and wonderful man preaching with such earnestness and urgency, and responds by saying, "Oh, I see, I see! Eternal life, eternal life!" At the very same time, the contrary and eccentric preacher put forth a fragrance that was foul to the one, and absolutely wonderful to the other. How amazing! This interesting man becomes the instrument in the hand of the Redeemer simultaneously sealing judgment in one hearer, and bringing forth life in the other.

The man who claims to speak for God but does not stir the minds of men to either anger or joy is not worth the paper upon which he writes his sermons. Furthermore, the man who is eccentric and contrary for the sake of having that reputation should consider work in other fields, for he will give an account to the Lord of the harvest for the wrong kind of foolishness that he displayed. Would to God that He would raise up true preachers of the Word who are willing to be fools for the sake of their Master. May they stand in the long line of eccentric preachers who have faithfully served the Lord. Moreover, may the men who come into contact with these unique fellows value the experience and take heed to the powerful things they say.

This is certainly the heart of the Prince of Preachers that comes bursting forth in the book that you now hold in your hand.

Ron Metheny has done a great service for the people of God by bringing Spurgeon's book back to modern readers in a fresh and updated form. I, for one, am very thankful for it, and I pray that you are as well. May you read it to your profit, and grow in your appreciation for The Eccentric Preacher.

Pastor Kyle Reeder
The Solid Rock Baptist Church
Benton, KY
Spring 2024

Spurgeon's Preface

I have published this little volume very much in self-defense. Some years ago I delivered a lecture on "Eccentric Preachers," and a reporter's notes of it were published in one of the newspapers. These, like all such things, were mere pickings and cuttings, and were by no means the lecture itself. Gentlemen of the press focus on grabbing the attention of their readers, and make selections of all the most notable stories, or intriguing quotes, used by a speaker, and when these are taken out of their context the result is anything but satisfactory. No man's speeches or lectures should be determined by a brief news article, that in any case is only a sketch, and in many instances is a gross caricature.

I thought no more of my lecture until the other day, when I ran across the reporter's rags and bones published in America as an address by myself, worthy to be bound up with my book on *Commenting and Commentaries* [see Appendix A, NOTE 0A]. Those notes were suitable for a newspaper, but I refuse to own them as my creation. It shocks me that the American editor failed to have corrected the more obvious mistakes of the reporter, such as calling Peter Cartwright "Peter Garrett," and Lady Anne Askew "Lady Askayne." Peter Cartwright was an American backwoods preacher, and his name should have been familiar to the American editor, but some publishers are so focused on releasing their books that they don't have enough time to proofread.

Discovering that I had in my possession the entire manuscript of the mutilated lecture, I considered printing it, to show what I had actually spoken; but on looking it over, I decided it would be better to expand it and turn it into a small book. I hope the reader will not be a loser by my decision.

I desire by this little volume to plead against the hypercritical spirit that makes a man a criminal for a word, and the lying spirit that spreads falsehood left and right, to the hurt and grief of the most zealous of my Master's servants. Many listeners lose a lot of blessing by criticizing too much, and meditating too little; and many more incur great sin by falsely accusing those who live for the good of others. True pastors have enough worries and concerns without being burdened by undeserved and useless faultfinding. We have something better to do than to be forever answering every malicious or frivolous slander that is flung our way. We expected to prove our ministry *by evil report and good report* (2 Corinthians 6:8 KJV), and therefore we are not overwhelmed by abuse as if it's something new that had happened to us; yet there are fragile, affectionate spirits who feel the ordeal intensely, and are sadly handicapped in brave service by cruel attacks. The rougher and stronger among us laugh at those who ridicule us, but on others the effect is very sorrowful. For their sakes, these pages are written; may they be a warning to malicious persons of little wit who defame the servants of the Most High God.

As ministers, we are extremely far from being perfect, but many of us are doing our best, and we are grieved that the minds of our people should be more directed to our personal imperfections than to our divine message. God has intentionally put His *treasure in jars of clay, to show that the surpassing power* should be attributed to Him alone (2 Corinthians 4:7). We emphatically ask our listeners not to be so occupied with the faults of the chest as to forget the jewel. *Wisdom is justified by all her children* (Luke 7:35), and grace works by such instruments as it pleases (cf. Romans 9:15-18). Reader, it is yours to profit by all my Master's servants (cf. 2 Timothy 3:16-17), and even by

Yours truly,

C. H. Spurgeon

Chapter 1

What Is Eccentricity?

Should I not be very timid in speaking on eccentric preachers when I am somewhat sarcastically requested by an anonymous letter writer to *look at home?* I do look at home, and I am glad that I have such a happy home to look at. Trembling has not overtaken me on receiving my nameless friend's advice, for two reasons: first, because I am not horrified by being charged with eccentricity, and secondly, because I do not consider myself to be guilty of that virtue or vice, whichever it may be. Years ago I might have been convicted of a mild degree of the quality, but since so many have copied my style, and such a considerable number have borrowed my sermons, I propose that I am rather the orthodox example than the glaring exception. After having lived for a quarter of a century in this region, I am no longer regarded in London as a phenomenon to be stared at, but as an old-fashioned kind of body who is tolerated as an established part of the ecclesiastical life of this vast city. Having moved in one orbit year after year without coming into serious collision with my neighbors, I have reason to believe that my pathway in the religious heavens is not eccentric, but is as regular as that of the other lights that twinkle in the same sky. I have probably done my anonymous correspondent more honor than he deserves in paying so much attention to him; indeed, I only mention the man and his correspondence that I might bear witness against all anonymous letters. Never write a letter that you are ashamed to put your name on; as a rule, only rude people are guilty of such an action, though I hope my present correspondent is an exception to the rule. Be so eccentric as to always be able to speak the truth to a man face-to-face. And now to our subject.

It is not the most profitable business in the world to find fault with our fellows. It is a trade that is generally pursued by those who would excuse themselves from self-examination by turning their censure on others. The log in their own eye does not appear to be quite so large while they can discover specks in other men's optics, and therefore they resort to the amusement of defamation. Ministers are the favorite prey of critics, and on Sundays, when they think it proper to talk religion, they keep the rule to the letter but violate its sense by most irreligiously overhauling the personalities, characters, sayings, and doings of God's servants. "Dinner is over. Bring the walnuts, and let us crack the reputations of a preacher or two. It is a pious exercise for the Lord's Day." Then tongues move with abounding clatter; tales are told without number, and when the truth has been exhausted, a few "inventions" are exhibited.

One person saw a preacher do what was never done, and another heard him say what was never said. Old fictions are brought up and declared to have happened a few days ago, though they never happened at all, and so the good people make the Sabbath holy with pious gossip and sanctimonious slander. There is a very serious side to this when we remember the fate of those who love to make up a lie; but just now we will not dwell on that solemn topic, so that we are not accused of *lecturing* our audience in more ways than one. So far as I am personally concerned, if the habit we are speaking of was not a sin, I do not know that I would care about it, since after having had more than my fair share of criticism and abuse, I am not one iota the worse for it in any respect; no bones are broken, my position is not injured, and my mind is not soured.

From the earliest period it has been found impossible for messengers whom God has sent to suit their style of utterance to the tastes of all. In all generations useful preachers of the gospel have been objected to by a portion of the community. Mere chips in the porridge [see Appendix A, NOTE 1A] may escape censure and subtly win the tolerance of indifference, but definite worth will be surrounded with warm friends and red-hot foes. He who hopes to preach so as to please everybody must be a newcomer to the ministry, and he who aims at such a target would do well to quickly leave its ranks. Men must and will criticize and object: it is their nature to do so. John came neither eating nor drinking. He was at the same time a Baptist and an abstainer, and nothing could be reported against his habits that were even remotely indulgent or luxurious; but this excellence was made his fault, and they said, *"He has a demon"* (John 10:20). Jesus Christ came eating and drinking, living as a man among men; and what they pretended to desire in John became an offense in Jesus, and they libeled Him as *a glutton and a drunkard, a friend of tax collectors and sinners* (Matthew 11:19). Neither the herald nor his Master suited the inconsistent tastes of their contemporaries. Like children playing in the marketplace, who would not agree on what game should be played, so were the sons of men in that generation. They rejected the messengers because they did not love the God who sent them, and they only pretended to object to the men because they did not dare admit their enmity towards their Master. As a result, the objections were often inconsistent and contradictory, and always frivolous and irksome.

Filled with the same spirit of contrariness, the men of this world still depreciate the ministers whom God sends to them and profess that they would gladly listen if different preachers could be found. Nothing can please them; their criticisms are dealt out with mindless ubiquity. Peter is too blunt, Apollos is too eloquent, Paul is too argumentative, Timothy is too young, James is too strict, John is too lenient. Nevertheless, *wisdom is justified by her deeds* (Matthew 11:19). At this time, when God raises up a man of originality who strikes out a course for himself and follows it with success, it is normal to accuse him of being eccentric. If his honesty may not be suspected, nor his zeal questioned, nor his power denied, then sneer at him and call him eccentric, and it may be the arrow that will wound.

Let us now pay attention to this dreadful word *eccentric*, and then see how it has been attached to certain preachers of the gospel, and those who are not the least in usefulness.

What does it mean to be eccentric? The short and easy method for determining the meaning of a word is to go to the dictionary. Dr. Samuel Johnson, What do you say? The sage replies, "It signifies deviating from the center, or not having the same center as another circle." The gruff lexicographer proves his definition by quoting from an astronomer who charges the sun with eccentricity. "By reason of the sun's eccentricity to the earth and obliquity to the equator, it appears to us to move unequally." Eccentric preachers are evidently in a brilliant society.

Now I am free to admit that the word has come to mean "peculiar," "odd," "whimsical," and so on; but by going a little deeper into its etymology, we discover that it simply means that the circle in which an eccentric man moves is not quite in accord with that which is followed by the majority. He does not keep to the conventional ring, but deviates more or less as he sees fit. It would be easy to prove that a movement may be eccentric and yet quite conventional and effective. Every man who works with machinery knows what it is for one wheel to be eccentric to another, and he also knows that this may often be a necessary and practical arrangement for the purpose of the machine. It does not seem so heinous, after all, that a man should be eccentric. I suppose the popular meaning is that a man is off the circle, or in more coarse language, off-kilter. But the point is, who is to tell us what is askew, and who is to decide which circle a man is bound to follow? It is true, this second circle is not concentric with the first, but it is not necessarily more eccentric than the first, for each one is eccentric to the other. It may be that circle A is eccentric to circle B, but circle B is just as eccentric to circle A. A man called me a Dissenter the other day, and I admitted that I dissented from him, but I charged him with being a Dissenter because he dissented from me. He replied that I was a Nonconformist, but I replied back that he also was a Nonconformist, since he did not conform to me. Such terms, if they are to be accurately employed, require a fixed standard; and in the case of the term *eccentricity*, we must first determine a center and a circumference from which to depart. This will be no easy task; indeed, those who attempt it will find it to be impossible in matters of taste and deportment, according to the old adage, "*de gustibus non est disputandum est*" ("in matters of taste, there can be no disputes"), and the well-worn proverb, "every man to his taste."

In morals, conscience has fixed the center and struck the ring; and in religion, revelation has used the compasses and given us a perfect sphere. God grant that we may not be eccentric towards God, either as to holiness or truth, for that would be fatal. But when trends and tradition mark off misshapen imitations of the circle of perfection, or even dare to impose curves of their own, it may be supremely right to be eccentric, since all the saints have walked an eccentric path as they have traveled the narrow way in the teeth of the many who pursue the downward road.

From such consecrated eccentricity come martyrs, reformers, and the leaders of the advance guard of freedom and progress. Breaking loose from the shackles of evil customs, such men first stand alone and defy the world; but before long, the great heart of humanity discerns their excellence, and then people are so eager to fall at their feet that the idolatry of hero worship is rarely escaped. To us these men seem more sublime in their solitary adherence to the right and to the true, than when they become the centers of admiration; their brave eccentricity is the brightest gem in their crown. The slavery of custom is as hard and crushing as any other form of human bondage, and blessed is he who for the truth's sake refuses to wear the annoying chain, preferring rather to be charged with peculiarity and put up with ridicule. It is clear, then, that eccentricity may in certain cases be a virtue. When it touches the moral and the spiritual it may be worthy of all honor.

As to preachers and their mode of procedure, what is eccentricity? Who is to fix the center? I say to all those self-proclaimed critics who tell us that certain preachers are eccentric, Who is to fix the center for them? Will this important task fall on those gentlemen who buy lithographed sermons and preach them as their own? These men are in no danger of violating propriety in the excess of their zeal, since their sermons are cut-and-dried for them at wholesale establishments. Do you ask, "Is this true?" I answer, "Undoubtedly it is."

Just the other day, to test the matter, I sent my secretary to a certain bookseller, and he brought specimens of these precious productions – lithographed or handwritten – home to me at prices descending from a shilling [approximately $40 U.S. (2024)] to sixpence [approximately $20 U.S. (2024)] each: an astounding variety, believe me. Some of these invaluable sermons are carefully marked in places to indicate the degree of emphasis to be used, and spaces or dotted lines are employed to indicate the pauses and their suggested length. No one calls the users of these pretty things eccentric; are we, therefore, to regard them as the model preachers to whom we are to conform? Are we all to purchase spiritual food for our flocks at the exorbitant price of half a guinea [approximately $410 U.S. (2024)] per quarter for thirteen sermons, to be exchanged at Lady Day, Midsummer Day, Michaelmas Day, and Christmas Day [see Appendix A, NOTE 1B]? If these things are so, and this trade is to be continued and increased, I suppose that we who think out our own sermons, and deliver them fresh from our hearts, will be regarded as oddballs, just as John Wesley was stigmatized as eccentric because he wore his own hair, when all the fashionable world was happy to wear wigs. Well, my brothers, if it is ever in fashion to wear wooden legs, I will be eccentric enough to stick with the legs that God gave me, weak as they are, and I trust that the number of eccentric people will be sufficient to support me.

Who is to fix the center of the circle? Should we place the compasses into the hands of the high-flying brothers whose rhetoric towers into the clouds and is shrouded and lost in them? These certainly dicker impressively, dealing in the sublime and beautiful just as freely as Edmund Burke himself. No layperson understands nor even dares to attempt to understand these gentlemen who are of the altitudes and profundities. Their big words are by no means necessary due to the solemnity of their subject-matter, but seem to be chosen on the principle that the less they have to say, the more pompous their phrases must be. In their rhetoric they

Set wheels on wheels in motion—such a clatter—
To force up one poor nipperkin of water!
Broad ocean labors with tremendous roar
To heave a cockle-shell upon the shore.[1]

---

1   Quatrain from the poem, On Johnson, written by English satirist John Walcot under the pseudonym "Peter Pindar"; Wells, 1905, p. 75

Mr. Muchado is still engaged in whipping his creams into a froth of the consistency of half a nothing; and we may hear Reverend Mr. Pretty-man in many pulpits exercising the art of spread-eagle to a clique who does not suspect him of eccentricity, but considers him to be the model divine.

These highfliers are not only comparable to masses of floating clouds in words, but are also equally beyond all comprehension in doctrine. They are philosophical gentlemen, superior persons of special culture, although what has been cultivated in them, except an arrogance of learning, would be hard to say. They confuse those whom they should confirm, and confound those whom they should establish. Bishop Blomfield tells us that a certain verger [church official] said to him, "Do you know I have been a verger of this church for fifty years, and though I have heard all the great sermons preached in this place I am still a Christian?" Now, are these dealers in words and dreams to fix the center? If so, we intend to be eccentric; and blessed be God we are not alone in that resolve, for there are others who join us in the opinion that to be studying the prettinesses of elocution, and the fancies of philosophy, while men are perishing around us, is the brutal eccentricity of a Nero, who fiddled while Rome was burning, and sent his galleys to fetch sand from Alexandria while the populace died from lack of bread. If the center is to be up in the clouds, let a few of us who care for something practical step down below and be regarded as eccentric.

It is an odd thing that some men prefer to speak on topics that they know nothing about, and from that, no benefit can possibly arise, while themes that might edify are disregarded. John Timbs [Spurgeon proceeds to paraphrase and quote a select portion of John Timbs's published work, *English Eccentrics and Eccentricities* (1866)] tells us of an eccentric "Walking Stewart," who had toured half the world but would never talk of his travels, preferring to ramble about "The Polarity and

Moral Truth" on which he spoke so wildly that no one could make heads or tails of it. Like this departed prominent person, certain men are most at home when they are all abroad, and are most important when their subject is insignificant. We do not choose their center, since it is far more suitable for will-o'-the-wisps than for ministers of the eternal Word. When all souls are saved and all mourners comforted, we may venture to discuss profound theories, but not while graveyards are filling up with those who do not know God.

Where, then, is the center to be found? Am I directed to that vestry over there? I beg your pardon – cloakroom. If you open that door, you will make out a considerable number of cupboards, presses, and recesses. Where are we? Is this a milliner's shop, or a laundry, or both? Those linen garments reflect great credit on the washerwoman and ironer; but the establishment is not a laundry, since black gowns, and white gowns, and raiment as fine as Joseph's coat of many colors hang here. And what a variety! Here, young man, go get the ecclesiastical dictionary! Here we have an alb and an amice, a cloak for the minister, and a linen cloth for the bread and wine, and – well, there's no end to the concerns! We are not well educated in the terminology of these clothing establishments, but we are informed that these things are not to be treated with flippancy, seeing that in them abides much grace that aids in the edification of the saints. In truth, we have little desire to linger among these resplendent rags, but assuredly if the center of gravity lies with gentlemen who adorn their physical bodies in this way, we prefer to be eccentric, and dress as other male human beings are accustomed to doing.

To us, it has even seemed necessary to discard the white necktie. When the white necktie was the everyday dress of a gentleman, it was all well and good; but now that it has grown to denote a dignitary of the clerical sort, or in other words, has become a priestly badge, it seems best to abandon it. This may be done more readily because it is also the favorite decoration of undertakers and waiters at hotels, and a minister has no wish to be taken for either of these respectable servants. Some young preachers delight in extremely long neckties, and others tie them with great precision, reminding us of "Beau" Brummel, who produced miraculous ties, because, as he said, he gave his whole mind to them.

I was greatly aided in the brief dismissal of my tie by an incident that happened to me when I first came to London. I was crossing the river by a penny steamboat, when a rude fellow said to me, "How are you getting on at Hitchcock's?" I could not imagine what he meant, but he explained that he assumed I was in the clothing line, and was probably at that eminent firm. He tried hard to find out where I was working, and when I offered in reply that I knew none of the houses in the city, and was not in the fashion industry, "Then," he said, "you're a Methodist minister"; which was a better shot by far, and yet not quite a bull's-eye. Having no desire to be lifted into the clerical order, or to claim any distinction above my fellow church members, I dress as they dress, and wear no special distinguishing mark. Let people of sense judge whether this is one-half so eccentric as arraying oneself so that it is hard for spectators to guess whether you are a man or a woman, and very easy to say that your attire is not manly, but ostentatious, and oftentimes gaudy and absurd. The center is not here. *Those who wear soft clothing are in kings' houses* (Matthew 11:8), but the King of Kings cares nothing for the finery and folly of religious parade.

According to word of mouth, the center of the circle is fixed by the dullest of all the brotherhood, because with many, to be eccentric means to have anything more than half a grain [see Appendix A, NOTE 1C] of common sense, or the slightest affinity towards humor. Have anything like originality, anything like genius, anything like a glimmer of wit, or anything like natural wholehearted action, and you will be called eccentric directly by those who are used to the gospel of humdrum. The concentric thing with many is to prose away with great propriety and drone on with supreme decorum. Your normal person says nothing that can by any chance offend anybody, and nothing that is likely to do anyone good. Devoid of faults, and destitute of excellencies, the proper preacher pursues his mechanical round, and shudders at the more erratic motions of real life. Far be it from us to depreciate the excellent brother, for his way is doubtless the best for him, yet there are other modes that are just as commendable though more likely to be censured. If you will be as dry as sawdust, as devoid of juice as the sole of an old shoe, and as correct as the multiplication table, you will earn yourself a high degree in the great university of Droneingen [see Appendix A, NOTE 1D], but if you wake up your soul and adopt an energetic delivery, and a natural, masculine, lively, forcible mode of speaking, then all the great authorities of that gigantic institution will say, "Oh dear, it is a pity he is so eccentric." Common sense decidedly objects to having the center for an eagle fixed by an owl, or the circle for a waxwork figure forced on a living man.

As to this supposed center of the circle that we have tried in vain to settle, it may be as well to remark that it is not fixed, and never can be fixed, for environments and times and circumstances involve perpetual change. Some hundred or more years ago John Wesley stood on his father's grave to preach in Epworth Churchyard, and he was thought very eccentric for proclaiming the gospel in the open air. As for George Whitefield, he was considered to be demented, or he would never have taken to the fields. Our Lord and His apostles had long before preached under the open heavens, and, persecuted as they were, no one in those days called them eccentric because of that particular practice; and, to show how the ideas of men have changed again, no one is now considered to be eccentric for open-air preaching, or at least, not in these regions. I might preach standing on a gravestone tomorrow, and no one would criticize me. Yes, I forgot, it must not be in a national graveyard, or I would be liable to something dreadful. We must neither stand on an Episcopal tombstone nor be laid under one with our own funeral rites. Those orthodox worms that have fattened on correctly buried corpses for so long would become ill if they fed on bodies over which the regular chaplain has not asked a blessing. This care for the worms is to my mind rather eccentric, but let that pass, for it will soon be counted among the superstitions of a dark age.

As times roll on, that which is eccentric in one era becomes ordinary and even popular in another. The typical and ordinary cut of a preacher of Queen Elizabeth's day would create a smile if it was to be imitated under the reign of Queen Victoria, and even the knee breeches, silk stockings, and silver buckles that I have seen on my respected grandfather would create many smiles if they were to reappear at the next meeting of the Congregational Union. "The nasal twang learned at the meetinghouse" was once regarded as the holy tone of piety, and yet the man who would use it now, if he was an Englishman, would be thought an odd being. Indeed, much of the oddity of the famous Matthew Wilks lay in that particular habit; he made you smile, even when speaking with all solemnity by the strangeness of his voice, and yet I never heard that our puritanical ancestors were anything but serious while listening to the same peculiar form of speech. There was a time when it was considered an outrageous deed of Jonas Hanway that he actually walked down a street in London on a rainy day, carrying a newfangled kind of round tent to keep from getting wet; yet no one quotes this action now as a proof of extreme eccentricity, since umbrellas are as common as mushrooms.

The following incident that happened to me will show the power of nationality and culture in producing the charge of eccentricity. A Dutchman, who from the very orderly style of his handwriting and the precision of his phrases, appeared to be quite an exemplary individual, once wrote me a sternly admonishing letter. From having read my printed sermons with great pleasure, he had come to consider me a godly minister, and, therefore, being in London, he took the opportunity to hear me in person. This he deeply regretted, however, since now he could no longer read my sermons with any enjoyment at all. What do you think I had said or done to deprive myself of the good opinion of such an excellent Hollander? I will relieve your mind by saying that he thought I preached exceedingly well, and he did not accuse me of any extravagant acts, but it was my personal appearance that shocked him. I wore a beard, which was bad enough, but worse than this, he noticed on my lip a mustache! Now this guilty thing is really so insignificant an affair that he might have overlooked such an unobtrusive offender. But no, he said that I wore a mustache like a carnal, worldly-minded man! Think of that. Instead of being all shaven and shorn like the holy man whom he was accustomed to hearing, and wearing a starched, ruffed collar all around my neck, about a quarter of a yard deep, I was so depraved as to wear no ruff, and renounce the razor. His great guy of a minister, with ruff and bands and gown and a woman's chin was not eccentric, but because I allowed my hair to grow as nature intended, I was eccentric and frivolous and carnal and worldly-minded, and all sorts of bad things. You see, what is eccentric in Holland is not eccentric in England, and vice versa. Much of the eccentric business is a matter of longitude and latitude, and to be quite correct one would need to take his bearings, and carry with him a book of costumes and customs, changed gradually according to the distance from the prime meridian.

Besides, we must not forget that as there have been times of persecution and times of toleration in religion, the same is true with the pulpit. In one era propriety ruled supreme, and men were doomed to instant ostracism if they stepped over the established line; while in another era a sort of Eccentric Emancipation Act was passed, and every man did what was right in his own eyes. At the present moment great longitude is allowed, and several people are now saying and doing very extraordinary things, and yet are escaping the charge of eccentricity. It has worked out well for them that some of us who lived before them were set in the stocks for having taken far smaller liberties. For myself, I venture to say that I have been severely criticized for anecdotes and illustrations of the exact same kind that I encounter in the very excellent sermons of my friend Dwight L. Moody, whom I appreciate probably more than anybody else. Many dear, good souls who have heard him with pleasure would not have done so twenty years ago, but would have regarded him as very eccentric. As to Ira Sankey's singing – of which I equally approve – would it not have been unpardonable even just a decade ago? Would Ned Wright and Joshua Poole, and brothers of that order, have been tolerated in 1858? According to the rules that judged Rowland Hill to be eccentric, I would say that these brothers are just as far gone, if not further, and yet no one hears an outcry against them for eccentricity. No, the bonds are relaxed, and it is perhaps possible that they are now too slack rather than too tight. It is, however, very curious to watch the moods of the religious public and see how what is condemned today is admired tomorrow. Such an observation has a great tendency to make a man rise above the verdict of the period, and choose his own path. To promote a masculine, courageous course of action in such matters is our main object in delivering this lecture.

If we are ministers, let us do what we believe to be most useful, and pay little attention to the opinions of our contemporaries. If we act wisely, we can afford to wait, for our reward is a higher commendation than that of men; but even if it was not, we can afford to wait. The sweeping censures of rash critics will one day be blown away like the chaff of the threshing floor, and the great heart of the church of God will beat true to her real champions, and clear their reputations from the tarnish of prejudice and slander. The eccentricity of one century is the heroism of another; and what is thrown out as foolishness in one age may be revered as wisdom ahead of its time in the next. It was well spoken by the apostle Paul: *With me it is a very small thing that I should be judged by you or by any human court. In fact, I do not even judge myself* (1 Corinthians 4:3).

To return to our circle and *con*centricity, it would be a great pity if the center of the circle could be fixed by an unalterable decree like that of the Medes and Persians. If we could settle once for all what is concentric and what is eccentric, it would be a grim evil, since the differences of speech and styles of delivery among God's ministers serve a most effective purpose. When Dr. John Owen said that he would give all his learning to be able to preach like the tinker, John Bunyan, he spoke unwisely, unless he intended nothing more than to extol honest John, since Owen's sermons – profound, solid, weighty, and probably heavy – suited a class of people who could not have received Bunyan's delightfully allegorical preaching of the plain gospel. No, Dr. Owen, you had best remain Dr. Owen, since we could by no means afford to lose that mine of theological wealth that you have bequeathed to us. You would have looked very awkward if you had tried to talk like the marvelous dreamer, and he would have played the fool if he had imitated you. It is pitiful to hear comparisons made between the different servants of the same Lord. They were made by their Master, the one as well as the other, and were set in different spheres to serve His own designs, and the same wisdom is displayed in each.

I heard the other day of a discussion that may have answered its design in educating youthful powers of debate, but intrinsically it was a trivial theme. It was this: Does the world owe most to the printing press or to the steam engine? The machines are both useful for the purposes intended, and both essential to the world's progress, so why contrast them? Why not also raise a controversy as to the relative values of needles and pins? Robert Robinson, of Cambridge, had a terse, vigorous, and somewhat homely style of preaching, and I heard it asserted that it was more effective than that of his successor, Robert Hall, who was to a great extent rhetorical and prodigious. Who is to judge in such a matter? Who in his senses would even tolerate the question? We claim for Robert Hall a master's seat in the assembly of preachers, and we would not place Robert Robinson beneath him, since each man suited the condition of the church. We admire every man in his own order, or even in his own disorder, so long as it is really his own. He has some end to serve in God's eternal purpose; let him answer that end without griping criticism from us. Who are we, that we should even condemn what seems to us odd and peculiar? How many souls were won to God by Rowland Hill's eccentricities, as they called them, the judgment day alone will reveal.

You have, doubtless, heard of the young man who was about to go to India, and a godly friend was very anxious that he should not leave the country in an unconverted state. He persuaded this young man to stay a week with him in London, and took him to hear a minister of great repute, a very able man – a man of sound argument and solid thought – in the hope that perhaps something that he said would lead to his friend's conversion. The youth listened to the sermon, pronounced it an excellent message, and that was the end of it. He was taken to hear another earnest preacher, but no result came of the service. When the last night came, the godly friend, in a sort of desperation, ventured with much trepidation to lead his companion to Surrey Chapel, to hear Rowland Hill, praying earnestly that Mr. Hill might not say any funny things; that he might, in fact, preach a very solemn sermon, and not say anything whatsoever that might cause a chuckle. To his horror, Mr. Hill that night seemed to be more than ever lively, and he said many humorous things. Among these he said that he had seen a number of pigs following a butcher in the street. At this he marveled, since swine typically have a will of their own, and that will is not often according to their driver's mind. Mr. Hill, on inquiring, found that the aforementioned pigs followed the leader because he had peas in his pocket, and every now and then he dropped a few before them, thus overcoming their scruples and propensities. In a similar way, said Mr. Hill, the devil leads ungodly men captives to his will, and conducts them into the slaughterhouse of everlasting destruction, by indulging them in the pleasures of the world.

The serious gentleman who had brought his friend to the chapel was greatly shocked at such an embarrassing analogy, and it grieved him to think of the flippancy his young friend would find in such a distasteful observation. They reached the door, and to his surprise the youth observed, "I will never forget this service. That story about the pigs has deeply affected me, because I fear it is my case." A happy conversion followed, and the critic could only retract his criticism in the silence of his own grateful heart. Well then, let each servant of God tell his message in his own way. To his own Master he shall stand or fall.

If God moves a Rowland Hill to talk about pigs, it will be better than if he had preached at length about babbling brooks, or blue-eyed seraphim. Taste may be shocked, but what of taste when men are to be aroused from the fatal slumbers of indifference? If you are living without Christ in the world, then your state and condition, in and of themselves, are far more shocking than any arousing words can possibly be. It is sin that is vulgar and in bad taste; so think those who can best judge – the purest of our race and the angels in heaven. It disgusts me to see a man whom God's Word declares to be *condemned already* (John 3:18ff) giving himself airs, and pretending to be too delicate to hear a straightforward remark from one who desires to save him from eternal wrath. He is coarse enough to despise the altogether lovely One, brutal enough to reject the gospel of love, and vile enough to rebel against his Creator and Preserver, and yet he is indeed a connoisseur in religion, and he picks over every word that is spoken to him for his good! This spiritual prudishness is sickening to the last degree.

I have shared the story of Mr. Hill because it is a type of many who are considered to be eccentric and coarse, but who are not so at all, except to shallow minds. There is nothing inherently vulgar in an allusion to pigs any more than to any other animals, since our Lord Himself spoke of *"throw[ing] your pearls before pigs"* (Matthew 7:6), and the apostle Peter alluded to the sow that was washed wallowing in the mire (2 Peter 2:22). Nor is there anything inherently coarse in the analogy of the hogs following the butcher; in fact, it is less coarse than Peter's metaphor that we have quoted, especially when coupled with the dog's returning to his vomit (cf. Proverbs 26:11). No creature, truly represented, is common or unclean. It is only a sort of pharisaism of taste that makes it so. Real vulgarity lies in immoral allusions and tactless innuendos, and these are to be found among men of dainty speech, such as Laurence Sterne, and not among holy and wholesome minds after the order of Rowland Hill. Paint your stories or your quotes with dirt, Mr. Slopdash, and we abandon you; nothing that is indecent can be endured in the service of a holy God. Come home to the heart in your own warm, homespun manner, and I, for one, will delight in you, Mr. Slapdash, and wish you Godspeed. There is so much difference between slop and slap that it might furnish a theme for a lecture, and yet there is only the change of a vowel in the words. In the same way, disgusting vulgarity and wholesome force wear the same outfit, and yet they differ as much as black and white. There is a charming poetry in many simple sayings that unsophisticated minds delight in. If a smile is raised, it only shows that the soul is awake, and is pleased to be taught so plainly. Critics may take out their penknives to gore and gash, but honest hearts delight in the natural expressions, the instructive comparisons, and the heartfelt statements of the sincere man whom the world labels an *eccentric preacher.*

Chapter 2

Who Has Been Called Eccentric?

In the previous lecture we gained some insight on the true meaning of eccentricity, and we discovered it in certain areas where it is least suspected, while we saw many to be free from it who have been widely charged with it. Let it not, however, be supposed that we shall attempt the justification of all eccentrics. We are sorrowfully compelled to concede to critics of the ministry that persons have entered it who have sadly disgraced our high calling. Men in all denominations have earned notoriety by being off-center morally and spiritually – these have deserved to be called eccentric in the worst sense. Now, while we stand up for the apostles, we expressly exclude Judas Iscariot. Find us a man who tries to attract attention by the false display of oddity, who is a mere charlatan or impersonator, and we do not have a word to say in his defense, but we give him over as a dead horse to the dogs of criticism. They may tear him to pieces, and devour him if they so desire, for impostors and pretenders deserve the critic's sharpest teeth. Find us a preacher who obtains notoriety for himself by descending to antics, and who goes out of his way to say sarcastic things and to make jokes on sacred subjects, and we decline to be his advocate.

Natural humor may possibly be consecrated and made to wear the yoke of Christ, but he who monkeys around with it is not a real man. If you find us a man who has a motive for what he says other than the glory of God and the winning of souls, he is the man who is off-center, and may we never enter his closet. And furthermore, if you discover a preacher who is indecent, and causes the cheek of modesty to blush, let him be cast out of the pulpit, and the door locked behind him. We have known men of the trash-mouth order who would have been nothing if they had not been offensive, and of these it may be said that they were worse than nothing when they followed their own style. There was nothing in their absurdities to excuse them, for they were not carried away by zeal, nor did the excellence of their subject-matter make up for the ridiculousness of their behavior. Of such men we will neither be defenders nor judges.

We do not care whether he performs in the parish church or hangs out at a little Bethel [see Appendix A, NOTE 2A]; the man who shocks decency and plays the fool with solemn truths is unworthy of his office. I have heard that a certain preacher, having traveled to Northamptonshire, among the shoemakers, in order to draw a congregation, advertised in the morning that he would in the evening tell them the quickest way to make a pair of shoes. When they crowded the place, he instructed them to take a pair of boots and cut the tops off. If this was actually done, then I say, let this comic among cobblers stick with what he knows best, but not go beyond his expertise. I had my doubts about this story, since I found it told both in reference to John Henley and Rowland Hill, and I was fairly certain that at least the second version was an old tale newly vamped; but I am sorry that I have run across an advertisement by Orator Henley that proves he actually did this, not in Northampton, but in London, and its headline was written in Latin to promote the event as something greater than what it was. We shall have more of this Orator Henley soon enough.

In my youth I remember the eccentric fame of a pastor who lived near my father's house. He found himself at church one Sunday morning with a political flier in his pocket instead of his sermon notes, and throwing it down into the churchwarden's pew, he ordered him to read a portion of it while he went home for his outline. Many highly questionable deeds were done by this preacher of the old fox-hunting school, and his most common behavior fully entitled him to be called eccentric. It would be a pity to revive the stories told in many an Essex village thirty years ago of ministers and clerks of a breed that ought to be quickly forgotten. Methodists and Ranters [see Appendix A, NOTE 2B] have been the song of the drunkard and the target of many flaming arrows, but never has anything been charged to the recklessness of their zeal that has been one tenth as mischievous as were the evil lives of those who opposed them. I do not care to say more; no section of the church can afford to throw stones, since no denomination has been free from unworthy ministers, adventurers, hypocrites, or downright fools.

Moderation is not the virtue of many. If one man casts a sprinkling of the salt of wit into his sermon, right away some half-idiotic brother must set the people grinning throughout the sermon. If one, to whom it is natural, is so carried away by his earnestness that at times his gestures become highly dramatic, immediately a certain crew begins mouthing and miming as if these things were the great power of God. If one man occasionally spiritualizes, yet stays within the bounds of discretion, they find it necessary to indulge all types of imaginations until one might say of them, as a foreigner said of King James's favorite preacher, "He plays with his text, patting it back and forth, like a cat does a mouse." They put the wise man's wig on their little skulls, and imagine that they have become as great as he is. These hangers-on of useful men have not even the virtue of being the genuine article; they are counterfeits exaggerating all the imperfections of the original, while omitting all the excellencies.

One can hardly tell from the distant past what to believe, and what to reject, of the character of Orator Henley, who flourished during the early to mid-eighteenth century in Butcher Row, Newport Market (London, England). If the representations of historians are correct, he was an eccentric man of the kind that disgusts all godly minds. He announced himself as "the restorer of ancient eloquence," and selected religious, political, and personal topics for his themes. He was frequently prosecuted for libel, and never seemed to bridle his tongue on that account, but with low crudeness and foolery he pursued the golden object that he had set before him. In an unfortunate moment he attacked the poet Alexander Pope, who in revenge held him up to scorn in his poem "The Dunciad" [*Book III*].

> Imbrown'd with native bronze, lo! Henley stands,
> Tuning his voice, and balancing his hands.
> How fluent nonsense trickles from his tongue!
> How sweet the periods, neither said, nor sung!
> Still break the benches, Henley! with thy strain,
> While Sherlock, Hare, and Gibson* preach in vain.
> Oh great Restorer of the good old Stage,
> Preacher at once, and Zany of thy age![2]

I say again that there is no knowing to what extent Henley deserved all this, but if reports are true, he was a mournful instance of talent perverted to evil uses, and of self-conceit

---

2   Three of Henley's preaching contemporaries: Bishop Thomas Sherlock (1678–1761), Bishop Francis Hare (1671–1740), and Bishop Edmund Gibson (1669–1748)

inflated to an amazing pitch. To such men the whip of scorpions – that Pope could handle so skillfully – was well applied.

Creatures of Henley's kind existed among the Friar Preachers of the medieval period, whose ignorance and cunning were equally the ridicule of their contemporaries, though even among them there were truehearted men whose peculiarities arose out of their zeal to do good. The genus of religious charlatans is not quite extinct at the present day, though seldom seen in such full development as in the friar period. Men of this order are generally known and accurately read by the Christian public, and seldom gain either profit or honor from their wretched adventure; it is a pity that they should.

The miserable instances alluded to are often used as stones to throw at really gracious men, and the attempt to prove that all preachers are alike is repeated in the face of a thousand facts. Because some charlatans have been eccentric, therefore all eccentric men must be mere impostors; and this being taken for granted, the next thing to be done is to represent really sober-minded men as wild and peculiar, so that they too may be regarded as deceivers.

A reputation for eccentricity has been unjustly fastened on many men by persistent falsehood. Throw enough mud at the wall, and some of it will stick – on this theory good men have been assailed. Whatever of originality and quaintness they have possessed has been grossly caricatured; and silly tales, the worthless legends of the remote past, have been revived and fathered on them. It is interesting to trace the pedigree of a pulpit story, although it is often not possible to discover its actual parent; in fact, we believe that, like Topsy [that is, a slave child (a fictional character) in the antislavery novel *Uncle Tom's Cabin* (1852) by Harriet Beecher Stowe], many of these tales have no father nor mother, but may say of themselves, "I suspect I grew." [In Stowe's original text, Topsy's response to

Miss Ophelia's question, "Do you know who made you?" actually reads, "I spect I grow'd. Don't think nobody never made me."] The rise and progress of a current falsehood, if well studied, would reveal a sad page in human history. The same anecdotes occur from age to age, but they are ascribed to different men.

In the days when hourglasses were attached to many pulpits, to suggest a limit to long-winded sermons, it was natural that slanderers should invent humorous stories concerning them. One of them is related in a sketch that depicts Hugh Peters preaching, and holding up an hourglass as he utters the words, "I know you are good fellows, so let us have another glass." It is probable that Peters never said this, and more than probable that if he did say something like it, his words were quoted out of context. Regardless, it was too good a story to let fall into disuse, and on this account, it was eventually told with slight variation about Daniel Burgess, a celebrated Nonconformist preacher, whose forceful speech frequently made him enemies. As if this wasn't enough, a very similar anecdote turned up a third time in a neighboring country, and this time it was a Presbyterian minister who used the expression, "Let us have another glass," when preaching before the High Commissioner. Fortunately for Rowland Hill and Matthew Wilks, the hourglass was out of style in their day, or else they would have been represented as saying the same thing. Liars should have good memories to recollect that they have already assigned a story to someone else. A speck of creative genius might also render their work a little less monotonous.

I remember reading with some amusement of Lorenzo Dow, who is reported some sixty years ago to have slipped down a tree in the backwoods, in order to illustrate the easiness of backsliding. He had previously pulled himself up with extreme difficulty, in order to show how hard a thing it is to regain lost ground. I was all the more distracted because it has so happened that this pretty piece of nonsense has been attributed to me. I was represented as sliding down the banisters of my pulpit – and *that* at a time when the pulpit was fixed in the wall and entered from behind! I never gave the falsehood a second thought, and yet it is repeated daily, and I have heard of people who say they were present when I did so, and with their own eyes saw me perform the silly trick. It is possible for a person to repeat a falsehood so many times that he at length imposes on himself and believes that he is stating the truth. Here is the original tale, extracted from William Taylor's book *The Model Preacher*:

A man once went to Vincennes (Indiana) in the United States, to hear Lorenzo Dow preach on backsliding. He said, "A large assembly of people gathered in the woods, and waited for Dow's arrival. Finally he made his appearance, and at the time when all expected the sermon, he arose, climbed up a smooth sapling, and cried out, 'Hold on there, Dow, hold on.' He soon slid down to the ground, and put on his hat and left. That was all the sermon we heard that day" [*The Model Preacher*, 1859, pp. 74-75].

If this was all the sermon, it certainly left a great deal for the hearer to work out, and it reminds us of the Welsh preacher who, with almost as little speaking, forcibly brought a great question before his people. He ascended the pulpit on a Sunday morning, looked around him and said, "My brethren, I shall ask you a question that neither you nor I can answer – What shall it profit a man, if he gains the whole world, and loses his own soul?" (cf. Mark 8:36 KJV). He then exited the pulpit, walked down the aisle, and went home. If the hearers did not think that morning, it was no fault of his. I am surprised no one has told this story about me; perhaps they think it too good.

It was reported of Rowland Hill that on one occasion having saved enough money to buy a chest of drawers, his wife used the saved amount to purchase a new bonnet. To punish her for this misappropriation of household funds, Mr. Hill is described as having exclaimed on the following Sunday, "Here comes Mrs. Hill with a chest of drawers on her head." It is truly amazing that this anecdote should have lived even for an hour, since Mr. Hill was of noble descent, and possessed considerable wealth and property. The purchase of any number of chests of drawers or bonnets would have been a matter of small consequence to him. Besides, he was so endeared to his wife, and a man of such excellent breeding, that no such language could have come from his mouth and been used by him under any supposable circumstances. When Mr. Hill heard of the story, he said, "It is an abominable untruth, derogatory to my character as a Christian and a gentleman – it would make me out as a bear." Across many of the stories that were printed concerning him, he wrote with his own hands the words, "A LIE," and truly there are others of us who might wear out our pencils in doing the same. Why are all these fabrications necessary? We have faults enough without attributing to ourselves more than we have committed. Men who are really eccentric furnish quite enough remarkable and peculiar incidents in the course of their lives, and if the actual peculiarities were criticized, there would be no room for complaint; but from where does all this delight in lies come?

It is necessary for a minister who is much before the public to be thick-skinned and to exercise to a very high degree the virtue of patience. It may help him if he will remember the conduct of good Cotton Mather, a man remarkable for the sweetness of his disposition. On one occasion, having taken a prominent interest in the political concerns of his country, he received a large number of abusive letters. All of these he tied up in a packet, and wrote on the cover, "Libels. Father, forgive them." No man of God should be astonished at slander, as though some strange thing had happened to him, since the best of God's servants have been subject to that trial. George Whitefield truly said,

"Thousands of prayers are put up for us, and thousands of lies are spread abroad against us." Of himself, concerning his tour in Scotland, they said, "Wherever he went he had an enormous crowd around him, and had the command to make them part with their money. He was a pickpocket, and went off to England with a full purse, but with a ruined reputation among all except his bigoted admirers." This was falsehood itself.

When young preachers are tested in this fashion, I ask them to recall the wise and weighty words of Thomas à Kempis [*The Imitation of Christ*, c. 1418–1427]:

> My son, do not take it grievously if some think ill of you, and speak that which you would not willingly hear.

> You ought to be the hardest judge of yourself and think that no man is weaker than yourself.

> If you do walk spiritually, you will not much weigh fleeting words.

> It is no small wisdom to keep silence in an evil time, and in your heart to turn yourself to God, and not to be troubled by the judgment of men.

> Let not your peace depend on the tongues of men; for whether they judge well of you or ill, you are not on that account other than yourself. Where is true peace and true glory? Are they not in God? And he that cares not to please men, nor fears to displease them, shall enjoy much peace.

From inordinate love and vain fear arise all disqui-
etness of heart and distraction of the mind.

Dr. Alexander Campbell once told me the following story:

On one occasion, when John Wesley was preaching, he said, "I have been falsely charged with every
crime a human being is capable of committing,
except that of drunkenness." He had barely uttered
these words before a miserable woman stood up
and screamed at the top of her lungs, "You old
villain, will you deny it? Did you not pawn your
wedding rings last night for a noggin of whisky,
and did not the woman sell them to our preacher's
wife?" Having delivered herself of this awful slander, the she-devil sat down amid a thunderstruck
assembly, whereon Mr. Wesley lifted his hands to
heaven, and thanked God that his cup was now
full, since they had spoken all manner of evil
against him falsely for Christ's name's sake.

After this we feel reconciled to the worthless tales that buzz
around us, annoying us for a brief moment, but doing no great
damage.

I would gladly hope that some untruthful representations
of good men are the accidental results of misreports. In these
days when reporters must furnish brief accounts of public
speeches, it is nearly impossible for them to do the speakers
justice, since in their hurry they hear inaccurately, and in their
brevity they give of necessity but a partial report. Now, the
omission of a single sentence may make a speaker appear very
absurd and eccentric. Of this we have a notable instance in the
case of our beloved friend Mr. C. A. Davis, of Bradford. His is

a sweet, poetical, well-balanced mind, and yet one would not think so from the newspaper report of a recent speech at our college meeting. He is reported to have said of us, "May every hair of your head be a wax candle to light you into glory, and may you be in heaven ten minutes before the devil knows you are dead." Assuredly this looks very outrageous as it stands, but let me personally vouch for its connection. Our friend said that he wished that he was able to express his love to us, and his heartfelt desires for us, and that he envied the enthusiastic ingenuity of a poor Irish woman who in thanking her benefactor exclaimed, "May every hair of your head, etc." Now, the reporter in this case was a friend to us all, but probably the crunch time of the printing office knocked out the previous sentences, and there stood the Catholic benediction in all its exuberance. I am somewhat amused that certain papers should abuse my brother Davis for this, since he is one of the most quiet, orderly, and correct speakers that I know, and I congratulate him on gaining a reputation for eccentricity by mere accident.

Do you not find it perplexing that some of us can never utter a playful sentence without being criticized? I would often speak informally to my dear friends, and unload myself, as a man might in the midst of his family, but

A young man's among you takin' notes,
And of course he'll print it.[3]

This is a sore oppression to a truehearted man who does not care to be forever under restraint. I sympathize thoroughly with Archbishop Tillotson when he said, "It is surely an uneasy thing to sit always in a frame, and to be perpetually on your guard; not being able to speak a careless word, or to use a negligent

---

3   Lines from the first stanza of Robert Burns's poem, "On Captain Grose's Peregrinations Through Scotland" (1789). Burns's original lines read in a parody of eighteenth-century Scottish slang: "A chiel's amang ye takin' notes, / And faith he'll prent it." Cunningham, 1866, p. 292.

posture without observation and censure. Nothing but necessity, or the hope of doing more good than a man is capable
of doing in a private station, can recompense the trouble and
uneasiness of a more public and busy life." The injustice of the
matter is that what a man does only once in a playful moment
– and what poor slave among us does not sometimes play? –
is bandied about as if it were a fair specimen of his whole life.
A man on a walk chases a rare butterfly, and immediately is
regarded as a mere boy who wastes his time in catching flies.
But is this fair? Is it not a practical lie? For my own part, I have
lived so long under a glass case, that like the bees that I have
seen at the Crystal Palace, I go on with my work, and try to
be indifferent to spectators; and when my personal habits are
truthfully reported, even though they are really not the concern
of anybody but myself, I feel utterly indifferent about it, except
in times of depression, when I sigh for a cabin in some vast
wilderness, where rumors of newspaper men and interviewers
might reach me nevermore. Would not some of our hearers be
rather more eccentric than their ministers if they were hunted
and reported as we are? May heaven spare them the affliction.

Here I depart to say that there should be greater caution
in believing silly stories about ministers of the gospel, and a
far greater reluctance to repeat them. They have enough to
endure without being made a laughingstock before the world,
for matters of which they are perfectly innocent. Taken as a
whole, they are probably less guilty of anything bizarre than
any other group of men. In fact, they are too inclined to freeze
into a cold, professional propriety; therefore it is foolish on all
accounts – by exaggeration and falsehood – to put a damper
on exceptional zeal simply because it is coupled with vivacity
of spirit and originality of style.

Still, there have been eccentric men, and names come to mind
where the epithet is appropriately connected. Who are they? I

will not dwell on Robert South, an accomplished preacher, some of whose sarcastic expressions are almost as compulsive as they are combative. I shall no more than mention such personalities as Dean Swift and Laurence Sterne, and I shall only allude to that witty and worthy person Reverend Sydney Smith, for these gentlemen, with all their genres, were not saturated with the gospel, and would scarcely care to be mentioned in connection with the honorable ones on whom I shall more extensively speak. Neither will I dwell on the eccentric persecutors who roared and raved against Methodists and revivalists from their pulpits, except that one of them deserves "honorable mention."

Samuel Roe, a Bedfordshire clergyman in the eighteenth century, and vicar of Stotfold, in that county, was a specimen of that inconsistent but not uncommon character, an enthusiast against enthusiasm. Without any extraordinary intelligence or accomplishments, he might have lived without notice, and died without remembrance, had he not brought attention to himself by a proposal for preventing the further growth of Methodism – a proposal as full of genius as it was of humanity. But this amicable and benevolent man will be heard in his own words: "I humbly propose to the legislative powers, when it shall seem appropriate, to make an example of the tent preachers, by enacting a law to cut out their tongues, as well as the tongues of all field teachers, and others who preach in houses, barns, or elsewhere, without apostolical ordination or legal authority" [Jacob Larwood, *The Book of Clerical Anecdotes or, the Antiquities, Humours, and Eccentricities of "the Cloth,"* 1871, p. 273].

I shall almost exclusively limit myself to good and true men who have really edified the church of God and led sinners to repentance.

To begin at the Reformation period, I must single out first and foremost grand old Hugh Latimer. The headdress he wore did not quench either his zeal or his wit. Is there any Reformer whose name strikes with such a familiar sound on the English ear as that of Latimer? We admire Thomas Cranmer, Nicholas Ridley, John Hooper, and the rest of them, but we love Latimer. There is something so genuine, and as we proudly say, so thoroughly English about that honest servant of God, that whether he kisses the stake in death or rebukes kings in his life, our hearts go out to him. Yet he was not only colloquial, but also at times so odd and whimsical in his speech that for a bishop he must be regarded as very eccentric. Did he not talk about that woman who suffered no sleep until she begged her companions to take her to the parish church, where she had so often slept through the sermon that she felt sure she would fall asleep there? Did he not tell his listeners an outlandish tale of the countryman who thought that Tenterden steeple was the cause of the Goodwin Sands [see Appendix A, NOTE 2C]? Listen to such talk as this:

> I will now tell you a charming story about a friar to refresh you. A limitour [that is, a friar who had a license to beg only within a given district, or whose duty was limited to a particular district for a certain period] of the Gray Friars [see Appendix A, NOTE 2D] preached many times, and had but one sermon on the Ten Commandments at all times. And because this friar had preached this sermon so often, one who had previously heard it told the friar's servant that his master was called Friar John Ten-Commandments. The servant informed the friar of this mockery, and advised him to preach on some other topic, because it broke the servant's heart to hear his master ridiculed. Now, the friar answered him saying, "Perhaps, then, you know the Ten Commandments well, seeing you

have heard them so many times." "Yes," said the
servant, "I assure you I do." "Let me hear them,"
said the master. Then he began: "Pride, greed,
lust," and so listed the seven deadly sins for the
Ten Commandments. And so there are many at
this time that are weary of the old gospel; they
would gladly hear some new things; they think
themselves so perfect in the old, when they are
no more skillful than this servant was in his Ten
Commandments. ["The Fourth Sermon of Master
Latimer's (Philippians 3:17-18)" in G. E. Corrie's
(Ed.) *Sermons by Hugh Latimer,* 1844, p. 524]

More colloquial still, if possible, is his talk about the various
cheats of his own day:

I will tell you of a false practice that was carried
out in my hometown. But I will not tell it to you
to teach you to do the same, but instead to despise
it, since those who use such deceitfulness shall be
damned world without end. I have known some
who had a barren cow, and they would gladly have
had a great deal of money for her, and so they go
and take a calf from another cow and put it with
this barren cow to market, pretending that this
cow had given birth to that calf, and so they sell
their barren cow for six or eight shillings higher
than they should have. The man that bought the
cow comes home; he conceivably has many children, and has no other cattle but this cow, and
thinks he will have some milk for his children. But
when all things come to pass, this is a barren cow,
and so this poor man is deceived. The other fellow

that sold the cow considers himself a happy guy, and a wise merchant, and he is called an enterprising person. But I tell you, whoever you are, do so if you wish, you shall do it at this price: you shall go to the devil, and there be hanged on the fiery gallows world without end.

I will tell you another false deed. I know that some farmers go to the market with eight bushels of grain. Now, they would gladly sell at a high price their worst, along with their best, and so they use this policy: they go and put a strike [see Appendix A, NOTE 2E] of fine barley or wheat in the bottom of their sack, then they put two strikes of the worst they have, then a good strike on top at the sack's mouth, and so they come to the market. Now, there comes a buyer, asking, "Sir, is this good grain?" "I assure you," the farmer says, "there is no better in this town"; and so he sells all the barley or wheat as the best, when there are only two strikes of the best in the sack. The man that bought it goes home thinking he has good grain. When he empties it all out of the sack, the strike that was in the bottom covers the bad in the middle, and so the good man will never perceive the fraud until he goes to use his grain. The other man that sold it sees this as policy, but it is theft in the eyes of God, and he is bound to make restitution for so much of those two strikes that were nothing and were sold at a high price. So much he ought to restore, or else he will never come to heaven, if God is true in His Word. I could tell you of another falsehood, how they make wool to weigh much, but I will not tell it

to you. ["The Fifth Sermon upon the Lord's Prayer,
Made by Master Hugh Latimer (Matthew 6:9)"
in *The Sermons of the Right Reverend Father in
God, and Constant Martyr of Jesus, Hugh Latimer,
Volume 2,* 1824, pp. 75-76]

Imagine the commotion if a right reverend father was to talk
like that these days. "Shockingly odd" would be the verdict of
both Canterbury and Winchester, and even of Sodor and Man.

Taking a huge leap and coming down to modern times, we
note the great evangelical revival under George Whitefield and
John Wesley, and we ask, Who is the eccentric man here? The
answer is that several might be so named, but John Berridge
of Everton would be chief among them all. What a lump of
quaintness that man was, but who thinks of him at the present moment without admiration? His portrait forces you to
smile, and you cannot read his letters without laughing; but
what power was on him to stir men's souls and lead them to
the Savior's feet. John Thornton once seriously admonished Mr.
Berridge because he had asked in prayer at Tottenham Court
Road that the Lord would give his people no stale bread, but
only that which was baked in the oven that day. I fail to see the
extreme impropriety of that prayer; but when Thornton says,
"You once jokingly informed me that you were born with a fool's
cap on; please, kind sir, is it not high time that it was pulled
off?" I agree with the question. Still I have more sympathy
with Berridge's answer: "A fool's cap is not taken off as easily
as a nightcap; one clings to the head and the other to the heart.
Odd things burst from me as abruptly as croaking does from a
raven." Berridge would have been unable to live if he had not
found a vent for his high spirits in witty sayings. He appears
to have had a delicate, candid soul that acted on its impulses
without fear of what observers might say. Yet he was ever ready

to confess his fault in the area of excessive flightiness, and on one occasion he traces it to his not being in the best physical health. This may seem very absurd, but it is not. I have known seasons when suffering from neuralgia or depression that my only hope of speaking at all has been found in taking off all the brakes, and allowing my mind to have full swing. The more my head has ached, the more I have indulged in humor, or I would not have been able to speak at all.

Here is the passage to which I referred; it is from one of Berridge's letters: "Laughter is not found in heaven; all are too happy there to laugh; it is a disease of fallen nature, and as such infested me sorely when sunk into the lowest stage of a nervous complaint. It forced itself on me without provocation, and continued with such violence as to completely overwhelm me; and nothing could check it but choking it, that is to say, filling my mouth with a handkerchief." Such fits were infrequent with him, although he was always radiant with smiles. I rather admire the courage of the man who could laugh when he was suffering so severely. The effect that the sight of Berridge produced on the very sober mind of Andrew Fuller is well worth mentioning. He says, "I greatly admired that divine aura, that at the same time mingled itself with Mr. Berridge's facetiousness, and sufficiently chastened it. His conversation tended to produce a frequent but guileless smile, accompanied with a tear of pleasure. His love towards Christ appears to be intense. The visit left a strong and lasting impression on my heart of the beauty of holiness – of holiness almost matured."

When I remember that there is credible information how in the space of about twelve months some four thousand souls were brought to Christ by his preaching, and how in the region where he once labored his name is still mentioned as that of a great saint, I feel that there was nothing in the eccentricity of Berridge of which he should necessarily be ashamed.

Rowland Hill, whom Berridge calls "Dear Rowley," was hard at work for his Master when the old vicar was going off the stage, and he did well to carry out the old man's advice – "Do not study to be a refined preacher: Jerichos are blown down with rams' horns. Simply look unto Jesus for preaching food, and what is wanted will be given, and what is given will be blessed, whether it is a barley or a wheat loaf, a crust or a crumb. Your mouth will be a flowing stream or a fountain sealed, according to your heart. Avoid all controversy in preaching, talking, or writing; preach nothing down but the devil, and nothing up but Jesus Christ."

With Rowland Hill we naturally associate Matthew Wilks, who kept the Tabernacle full while Mr. Hill crowded Surrey Chapel. Concerning both of these we hope to speak more extensively further on. America in her formative years produced backwoods preachers of a rarely eccentric order, such as Jacob Gruber, William "Billy" Hibbard, James Oxley, Peter Cartwright, and others of a brave fraternity of men who labored with the ax in their hands and the gospel on their ready tongues. The same country also gave us Edward Thompson Taylor, the sailor preacher of Boston. However bizarre some of these men may seem, we cannot but admire their readiness for service and their insurmountable courage. Imagine going to a call as an itinerant preacher where the people write, "Be sure and send us a good swimmer, because he will have to cross an endless terrain of rivers with no bridges." "George," said Bishop Asbury to George Roberts, "where are your clothes?" "Bishop, they are on my back." Instead of a change of garments, this man carried a needle and thread in case his one set of garments accidentally ripped. We cannot be in favor of Peter Cartwright's propensity for physical violence. We trust it will remain a peculiarity confined to America for a preacher to be equally ready to fight or to preach. Some men may be all the better for being knocked down, but the knocker down will surely be all the worse. However, these members of the church militant were rough men dealing with rough men, and we are glad that we are not tempted in the direction of fistfights.

The Baptists, among many other less notable denominations, have had Robert Robinson, of Cambridge, of whom Robert Hall said that he could say "what he pleased, when he pleased, and how he pleased," and John Ryland, of Northampton, whose natural force and spontaneity sometimes carried him into eccentric territories.

Among the Methodists have sprung up William Dawson, Gideon Ouseley, Squire Brooke, and others whose names will not soon be forgotten. Now, it strikes me that if we were bound to make out a short list of sincere and successful soul winners, we might be content to take the list that we have already made out. To say the least, it is remarkable that eccentricity and usefulness often go together. As it turns out, these extremely eccentric people, who are so frequently condemned, have nevertheless been among the most useful men of their times. Matthew Wilks's way of meeting objections to his whims and oddities was not a bad one. I am told that a delegation of his friends waited on the old gentleman to take issue with him for his irregularities of speech; he was shocking many good people, and his advisers hoped that he would endeavor to change. He said, "Well, gentlemen, if you have said what you have to say, I will ask you to wait just a minute or two while I run upstairs." Mr. Wilks went upstairs and brought down a long roll of paper that he unfolded with due dignity. "Look at that," he said. Yes, they looked at it. "Do you see the number of names?" he asked. "Yes," they answered. Then he said, "Here is another roll for you. Look at this! Count those names! Here is number three, look at this! Now, gentlemen, you see all these names? Well then, all these precious souls profess to have found the Savior and everlasting life through what you are pleased to call my whims and oddities; and if you will find a longer roll in the hands of those who have no such whims and oddities, I will try and alter my ways to please you; but until then, I shall certainly follow my own course." Common sense declares Mr. Wilks to have been right. We do not say that the end justifies the means, but we would venture to hint that means which have such an end need very little justification.

Let those whose barren ministries are as proper and respectable as a row of gravestones complain of the oddities of those who bring thousands to Christ. As for us, we have no heart for faultfinding, and only wish – without imitating their eccentricity – to discover the secret of these men's success, if by any means we might save some. Eccentric or not eccentric will matter little to us so long as men are delivered from the wrath to come and are led to trust in Jesus by the Word that we preach.

Chapter 3

Causes of Eccentricity

W e have continued talking about eccentric men, but we have not yet decided what it is that makes a man eccentric. Let us now come to the point. Some ministers have been reckoned eccentric simply and only because *they have been natural.* They have been themselves, and not copies of others; what was in them they have not restrained, but have given full play to all their powers. Take for instance John Berridge. Berridge was unusual by nature. In the former lecture I purposely quoted from his letters rather than from any of his sermons or doctrinal works, because in a letter you see a man at ease. Berridge could not help being peculiar, since the form of his mind led him in that direction, and his bachelor life helped to develop his idiosyncrasies. His uniqueness was all his own, and you see it in the management of his household, for instance, when he says to a friend,

> I am glad to see you write of a visit to Everton. We always have plenty of horse fodder on hand, but unless you send me notice beforehand of your coming, you will have a cold and paltry meal, since we roast only twice a week. Let me have a line, and I will give you

the same treat I always gave to George Whitefield, an eighteen-penny barn-door fowl. This will neither burst you nor ruin me; you will enjoy half at noon with a pudding, and the rest at night. Much grace and sweet peace be with you and your spouse; and the blessing of a new heart be with your children.

With many thanks, I remain your affectionate servant,

J. B.

Nor is it less evident in his hymns, even the most solemn of them; for instance, in the well-known verse where he speaks of the saints in heaven and he cries,

> Ah, Lord, with feeble steps I creep,
>> And sometimes sing and sometimes weep;
> But strip me of my house of clay,
>> And I will sing as loud as they.[4]

We are not likely to censure the good man for his oddities more severely than he does himself, since in another of his pieces he writes,

> Brisk and dull in half an hour,
>> Hot and cold, and sweet and sour;
> Sometimes grave at Jesus' school,
>> Sometimes light and play the fool.

> What a motley wretch am I!
>> Full of inconsistency!
> Sure the plague is in my heart,
>> Else I could not act this part.[5]

---

4   John Berridge, "The White-Robed Band" (c. 1785), fifth stanza.
5   John Berridge, "Inconstancy" (no date), fourth and fifth stanzas.

Rowland Hill, again, was odd by nature, and though he put great constraint on himself, his oddity would still break out. On one occasion he preached in Dr. William Bengo Collyer's chapel [see Appendix A, NOTE 3A] at Peckham, where everything was most prim and proper. He spoke for twenty-five minutes in a strain of deepest solemnity, but at last the real man broke out, and for the next fifteen minutes oddities came to the forefront. In the vestry, at the close, he observed that he had over and over again resolved to voice no expression that could excite a smile, but he said, "I find it's of no use. Though my very life depended on it, I could not help myself." He never went out of his way for odd and sensational sayings, he even sought to avoid them; but they were natural to him, and he was not himself without them. Do we blame the man for being himself? We do not blame him, but commend him. Originality is not to be censured but encouraged. Sir Joshua Reynolds says of painters, "Few have been taught to any purpose who have not been their own teachers." The excellence of Thomas Gainsborough was that he developed his own style in the fields, and not in the studios of an academy. "The methods he used for producing his effects had very much the appearance of an artist who had never learned from others the usual and regular practices belonging to the art; for still, like a man of strong intuitive perception of what was required, he found out a way of his own to accomplish his purpose." We need in the pulpit more Gainsboroughs, since we have quite enough of the academy men of this school and the other.

Cold-hearted professionals follow each other in tow, like those caterpillars I have seen at Mentone that make a procession head to tail in a straight line, until you half imagine it is only one single insect. But the man who serves his God with his whole heart is apt to forget his surroundings, and to fling himself so completely into his work that the whole of his nature comes into action, and even his humor, if he is possessed of that faculty, rushes into the battle.

Some men have been dubbed eccentric because they have been more truthful than their contemporaries. Exact truth-telling is not very common in our country. Few say that they are busy and cannot see those who call on them, but they are "not at home." Writing to people whom they hate, many begin with, "My dear sir"; and to people for whom they have no respect they subscribe themselves, "Your obedient servant." These are only quoted as tired, old illustrations of genteel falsehood, but like straws they show how the wind blows.

Now there are a few men who are called eccentric because they do not believe in polite lying, but speak the truth whether they offend or please. A gentleman not long ago was seen as very eccentric because when asked whether the tea was to his taste, he replied that it was not, since it was very weak and nearly cold. Others had sidestepped the question, or had expressed themselves delighted with the nauseous decoction, and none of these were seen as eccentric. It is a pity! Where truth is thought to be eccentric, the age itself is out of gear.

Edward Taylor presided at a prayer meeting among his sailor converts, and a great man from the city came in to honor the poor people with his presence, and to patronize their missionary. He made a speech in which he extolled the kindness of the wealthy Christian people of Boston in helping to build Taylor's chapel, and assisting in his support. He praised these superior people for their great consideration of poor degraded sailors, and he gave the audience a sufficient allowance of condescension to last them for the next six months at the least. As soon as the great man had finished, Taylor quietly asked, "Is there any other old sinner from uptown who would like to say a word before we go on with the meeting?" The eccentricity of that expression lies in the truthfulness by which it rebuked the impertinence of the speaker.

Good William Grimshaw of Haworth once displayed his

eccentricity when George Whitefield was preaching in his church. Whitefield in his sermon, having spoken severely of those professors of the gospel who, by their loose and evil conduct, caused the ways of truth to be evil spoken of, intimated his hope that it was not necessary to expand much on that topic to the congregation before him, who had long been privileged to listen to the earnest addresses of such an able and faithful preacher. Mr. Grimshaw got up and said in a loud voice, "Oh sir, for God's sake, don't talk like that; I beg you, do not flatter them. I fear that most of them are going to hell with their eyes wide open." This was very different from the smooth-talking flatterer who did not desire the visit of an evangelist, because it was only proper for evangelists to preach to the wicked, and he was unaware of any wicked people in his church.

Rowland Hill once rebuked an Antinomian who was in the habit of drinking. The man replied with an air of arrogance, "Now, do you think, Mr. Hill, a glass of spirits will drive grace out of my heart?" "No," said the faithful old gentleman, "since there is none in it." This was expressing the truth pretty plainly, and for that very reason it is spoken of as eccentric.

Matthew Wilks stood out for his hatred of flattering terms that certain fawning brothers would every now and then lavish on him. "There," he said, "I have been very pleased with my people's prayers tonight. No fluff, no flattery, no speaking of me as a dear, venerable saint until I almost go into hysterics. Saint, indeed! A poor worm! I can barely keep from shouting, when such language rattles my ears." To a wealthy man who had headed a subscription list for an excellent institution with a very small amount, he said, "I will have nothing to do with it since you do so little for it. You have strangled the child at its birth, when you should have nourished and cherished it until you had set it on its feet."

Now, in these cases the eccentricity lies in plain speaking, and this is an order of eccentricity of which we certainly cannot have too much, if it is accompanied by sincere affection and tempered with gentleness. But of this I feel quite sure, that if any man will make up his mind that he will only say what he believes to be strictly true, he will be thought odd and eccentric before the sun goes down.

Certain preachers have been very eccentric because *they have been masculine,* too masculine to be hampered by the customs and manners of the period. They have broken one rule after another that has been constructed for the propping up of mannequins, and have behaved themselves as men. Thomas Binney was often thought eccentric for nothing else but his boldness and freedom from pulpit affectations. Why sirs, there are places where it would be eccentric to speak so as to startle the drowsy; eccentric to stress your words by proper measure; eccentric to use a simple illustration; in fact, eccentric to speak anything more shocking than the polished trivialities of John Blair. Truehearted men are not willingly held in by the cramping irons of childish fashion, but they are of the mind of Matthew Wilks who said, "Flesh will cry out, 'What will men say?' but a sanctified conscience will cry, 'What will God say?'" Egyptian art was reduced to an unchanging ugliness by laws that fixed the form of every feature and limb of its statues. The artist who should have anticipated the graceful life of Grecian sculpture would have been condemned by his nation as unbearably eccentric, and yet unbiased ages would have exonerated the innovator from any fault. The case is the same with preachers who break through artificial rules, and boldly refuse to be mere imitators of socially acceptable norms. In some places the style has been fixed by some venerated pastor who has gone to his rest; his threadbare mantle, that was an excellent fit for him, is supposed to be the exact garment for his successor, and the old housekeepers of both sexes cry out against any who choose to wear their own clothes.

It is easy enough among Dissenters to find regulations as rigid as could be invented by any bench of bishops; you may not vary the length of the hymn or the order of the service by a hair's breadth, or you will sin against your own reputation and the feelings of the conservative portion of the congregation. There are few such places now, but more than enough, and, where the evil rules, the good folks are as tenacious in their established nonsense as ever the Church of England can be of her printed prayers and rules; and the preacher must submit to all the regular rubbish as if it were Scripture itself, or be pronounced eccentric and lacking in decorum. A man that is a man will yield for the sake of peace as far as his soul is unhampered, but beyond that he will ask, "Who makes these regulations, and to what end are they made?" Finding them to be worthless and injurious, he will put his foot through them, and there will be an end to the rubbish.

Some congregations are dying of dignity, and must be aroused by real life. People said that Rowland Hill rode on the back of order and decorum, and therefore he called his two horses by those names, so that if he could not ride on the back of them, he might make the saying nearly true by being dragged behind them. Order and decorum, in some of our churches, have manifested themselves to be deadly sins: dead and burying the dead (cf. Matthew 8:22 and Luke 9:60). Some congregations are so orderly to an extreme that they are like a vault in which the corpses lie, each one in due place, and no one dares to move or raise a voice loud enough to be called a chirp. This will not do. Bring the trumpet! Sound a blast and wake the sleepers! Eccentric! Yes, eccentricity, if you like to call life by that name. Heaven knows it is sadly lacking.

After all, the eccentricities of masculine life never equal those of the wretched dance (that is, death, or the sleep of death) that is so dear to mere routine. Think of such an event as the following happening among your orderly readers of other men's sermons, for the like has happened and must have happened many times. A certain preacher delivered a sermon that had a passage like this: "On account of your sins, and your neglect of the house of God, your unruliness and your gluttony, the anger of the Most High is provoked, and as a consequence this great plague has come upon you, and death is raging in every street." When the sermon was finished, the officials of the township wanted to know where this plague was, and what deaths had happened; indeed, all the congregation were anxious to know where this dreadful disease was raging. "Oh," said this orderly reader of sermons, "I do not know where it is, but it was in my sermon, and so it was necessary that I read it to you." It would be easy enough to expand upon the accidents that must occur where borrowed – or rather stolen – sermons are preached, but this is not my point; I merely mention this as one possible instance in which humdrum routine becomes itself ludicrous. To me it always seems ludicrous if looked at through the glass of truth. Primness, trendiness, and dignity are but a short distance from the ridiculous; at their very best there is but one step between them, and that step is often taken with complete obliviousness that it is so.

I venture to say that some men have been called eccentric because *they are really in earnest,* and earnestness defies rules. I do not believe that it is possible for a man in downright earnestness to be always *proper.* I suppose there is a proper way of getting a lady out of her bedroom when her house is on fire, but doubtless our firemen often violate the proprieties when they have to do such a thing. They have to rush in by any means possible to save life, and they cannot wait around to make apologies. The flames are urgent, and so the rescuer must also be urgent, or life will be lost. I suppose there is a proper way of pulling people out of the water when they are drowning, but I have known brave fellows who drag them out by the hair of their heads; this was rough and rude, but it achieved the purpose. Did anyone ever blame the doer of the deed for his roughness? Is not the soul more precious than the body, and who would permit it to be lost for the sake of etiquette? A man may go into the pulpit as prim as you please, and he may even wear tight-fitting lavender gloves, like I have heard of; but let him feel an inward anguish for the souls of men and he will forget his dignity and rip his gloves, and in all probability never buy a second pair. A man may be stiffly proper, and even elegant and delicate until he comes to real grips with men's consciences, and then, like the soldier at Waterloo who wished to be in his shirtsleeves, he will feel hampered by his rigidity and his formality, and will speak like a man to men, and then some fool or other will hold up his hands and cry, "Dear me, how dreadfully eccentric!"

A few preachers have appeared to be eccentric because of the wealth of poetry present in their speech. Men of the average school are somewhat startled by expressions that to poetic minds are natural enough, and by no means peculiar. It requires genius in the hearer to enjoy genius in the preacher. One of my personal friends, whose sermons are essentially poems, laughed heartily the other day at the expression of an admiring listener who at one time did not appreciate him. "I am very sorry that I foolishly left your ministry for a time," said the good man, "but then, you see, I used to hear you with a jaundiced eye!" It is this jaundiced eye of cold matter-of-factness that is unable to perceive the beauty of sparkling metaphors and illustrations, and therefore sees instead mere eccentricity.

In my earlier days I heard rustic prayers that thrilled me, not only with their spirituality, but also with their poetry, and yet I heard others exclaim against the extravagance of the language. One whom many regarded as eccentric in his preaching was a great favorite of mine, and I remember now his scintillating sayings, his choice aphorisms, and his rare imagery, while other sermons have faded from my memory because they never touched my heart. I could have said of him what John Bradford said of Hugh Latimer: "I have an ear for other preachers, but I have a heart for you." Doubtless there are many others who are condemned for their eccentricity by the simpletons around them, because they have prolifically creative minds, and they scatter pearls with both their hands.

Eccentricity has also been charged on *men of shrewd common sense.* They have baffled those who sought to entrap them, and, in revenge, their adversaries have dubbed them eccentric. They were nowhere near as gullible as their contemporaries, but leveled a little natural wit at egotists, hypocrites, and deriders, and so they must be libeled as odd fellows. As this is a point that I do not intend to dwell on at any length, I will only illustrate it by the story of the eccentric shepherd, and remark that similar shrewdness on the part of ministers is of the utmost value, but is pretty sure to incur the charge of eccentricity. Here is the story.

"An exceptionally proud minister, riding over a common, saw a shepherd tending his flock, and wearing a new coat. The preacher asked in a condescending tone who gave him that coat. 'The same people that clothe you – the church,' said the shepherd. The minister, a little miffed, rode on murmuring a considerable way, and eventually sent his servant back to ask the shepherd if he would come and live with him, since he thought of keeping a fool. The servant went to the shepherd accordingly and delivered his master's message, imagining that his master really wanted a fool. 'Are you going away then?' said the shepherd. 'No,' answered the other. 'Then you may tell your master that his salary won't support three of us,' replied the shepherd."

Rowland Hill and others were quite capable of giving such crushing replies to hypocrites and mockers, and, consequently, they did well to silence them, but it earned them the title of *eccentric.*

Some men have been eccentric on account of *the vast amount of dramatic energy with which they have been endowed.* Certain people, when they talk, match the action to the word from the force of nature and habit. It is in their makeup to be dramatic. Look at a Frenchman, how he speaks with his hands, his shoulders, his eyebrows, his feet, and his whole body. Very few Englishmen are dramatic in this way, but every now and then we may come across people who are just as energetic in that manner as the liveliest of our Gallic neighbors. And why not?

The famous William – or as the public delighted to say, "Billy" – Dawson, was nothing if not dramatic. I have heard a well-known minister say that Dawson was once preaching about Noah's ark, and finding himself boxed up in the pulpit he said, "This won't do." He opened the pulpit door and he came down the stairs to the bottom of the pulpit, and there he began to fell trees and saw logs, and then he seemed to be hammering away to make the ark, which was represented by the pulpit. This ark was built before them all, and the people were worked up to an intense excitement as Dawson continued to cry, "A flood is coming. I am making this ark for the saving of my house. There is no hope for anybody but those who come into the ark." Then he seemed to be boiling a great cauldron of asphalt, until he took his long brush and sealed the ark inside and out; and when all was done, his ship was there on the dry land, and like Noah he turned around and asked the people once again whether they would come into it and be saved. They would not come in, and so he declared he would go in alone. He went up into the pulpit and shut the door with the words, *"And the Lord shut him in"* (Genesis 7:16). Then came the flood, and our informant said that he felt as if the floor of the chapel erupted and the water began bubbling from below, while a torrential downpour came from above; and there was Dawson, another Noah, alive and safe, crying out that it was now too late, because the door was shut.

All were astonished and filled with breathless attention as he urged them to remember that such would soon be the case, and he preached unto them Jesus as the only salvation. None of us would attempt this, but neither would I have laid a finger on Dawson. Why should he not depict the scene in his own way? If God gave him the theatrical faculty, why should he not use it to impress his listeners? Perhaps he knew that those who were around him could not be impressed in any other way. This was the man who on another occasion described David and Goliath. He represented David emerging with his sling, and the giant boasting that he would give his flesh to the birds of the air and to the beasts of the field, and so on; but David replies, *"You come to me with a sword and with a spear and with a javelin, but I come to you in the name of the LORD of hosts"* (1 Samuel 17:45). He placed his stone carefully in the sling, whirled the sling in the air, and you could hear the stone whizzing towards the giant's brow. Just then Sammy Hick, the village blacksmith, who was sitting near the preacher, rose up in tremendous excitement and cried, "Now then, Billy, off with his head!"

For my part, I only like dramatization when it's kept in check and done thoroughly well. You have probably seen John B. Gough do that sort of thing admirably in his lectures. Have I not seen him walk what seemed to me miles while he was delivering one of his messages, rushing over the plains and through the rivers, and at last up the sides of Vesuvius after an eruption? I think I see him now, with his feet sinking in the hot ashes, struggling in vain and perishing before our eyes. It was grandly done, and no one had a right to object to it. Gough has caught David Garrick's idea, and speaks of truths as truths, making them visible before our eyes. I know the criticisms that are so easy to make about theatrical displays, dramatic performances, miracle plays, and so on, and I know also the real dangers that surround the practice; but I would far rather incur all the supposable perils than altogether banish such an awakening force from the pulpit.

Sometimes men have been regarded as eccentric because *they have been practical.* The occasion has demanded what in other circumstances would have been unjustifiable, and others not knowing the particular conditions have set their words and actions in another light, and made them seem objectionable. They intended to save men's souls somehow, by the blessing of God, and as a result they resolved to do anything and everything by which they could get at the indifferent, ignorant, and apathetic; and for this reason the things that they did have been outlandish and startling, but not more so than the need required. Such peculiar words or actions have been divorced from the circumstances out of which they grew, and put aside from the connection. The design of the preacher has been forgotten, and then the thing that has been done has seemed to be eccentric at least, if not censurable, although, mind you, had you yourself been there, and had you possessed the preacher's ready wit and intense earnestness, you most likely could not have done better. Let me give you one or two instances, and the first is from James Grant's sketch of Rowland Hill in *The Metropolitan Pulpit: Or, Sketches of the Most Popular Preachers in London, Volume 1.* It is told in a somewhat wordy style, but the change from my more abrupt manner may be a relief.

A pious woman, a member of Surrey Chapel, was married to a husband who, though kind to her, had no sense of religion; all the hours she spent devoted to hearing the preaching of the gospel, he delightfully spent in drinking beer. It so happened that the couple, through some disappointment in business, had been unable to pay their rent on a particular quarter day. Consequently, a seizure order on their furniture was put in place, and a party was employed, as the technical phrase has it, "to take possession." After turning over every possible scheme in their minds that might aid in extricating themselves from the difficulties in which they were involved, they were about to despair, when the idea occurred to the wife of submitting the circumstances of the case to Rowland Hill. She accordingly went to his house, at once got access to him, and rather nervously made a short and simple representation of the current state of affairs.

"How much would you require to save your furniture and get rid of the person in possession?" asked Mr. Hill.

"Eighteen pounds, sir, would be more than sufficient for the purpose," answered the poor woman, with a palpitating heart.

"I'll make you a loan of twenty, and you can repay me at your convenience. Send your husband to me when you get home, and I will have two ten-pound notes ready by the time he arrives. I prefer to give the notes to him rather than to you."

The woman left Mr. Hill's house and hurried home with light foot, but with an even lighter heart. Having communicated to her husband what had taken place between herself and her minister, it is needless to say that he lost no time in going to the house of Mr. Hill. The latter received him in a kind manner.

"And so," Mr. Hill said, "you are so unfortunate as to have a person in possession."

"We unfortunately have, sir," the husband replied.

"And twenty pounds will be sufficient to get rid of him and restore your furniture to you?"

"It will, sir."

"Well then," said Mr. Hill, pointing to the table, "there are two ten-pound notes for you, that you can repay when you are able. Take them."

The husband went to the table, took the notes, and was in the act of folding them up, at the same time warmly thanking Mr. Hill for the act of friendship he had done for him, and expressing a hope that he would soon be able to pay the amount back, when the gentleman suddenly exclaimed, "Wait a minute! Just lay the notes down again until I ask a blessing on them."

The husband did what he was told, at which point Mr. Hill, extending both his arms, said a short prayer to this effect: "Oh Lord, who is the Author of all mercy and the Giver of every good and perfect gift, may You be graciously pleased to bless the sum of money that is given to he who is now before You, that it may contribute to his present and eternal welfare. For Jesus Christ's sake."

"Now sir," said Rowland Hill, as he finished his brief supplication, "now, sir, you may take the money."

A second time the man picked up the two ten-pound notes, and was folding them up like before, when Mr. Hill interposed by reminding him that he had forgotten one thing. It may be easily supposed that by this time the man was a good deal confused. His confusion was increased a hundred percent when Mr. Hill remarked, "But, my friend, you have not asked for a blessing on the money yourself. You had better do it now."

"Sir," faltered out the husband, barely able to support himself, "sir, I cannot pray. I've never prayed in all my life."

"You have more need to begin now," observed the gentleman, in his own cool yet rebuking manner.

"I cannot, sir; I do not know what to say."

"Try, try and thank God; ask His blessing, however short your prayer may be."

"I cannot, sir; I cannot say a single sentence."

"Then you can't have the money. I will not lend twenty pounds to a prayerless man."

The man hesitated for a moment, and then with closed eyes, and uplifted hands, he said with great earnestness, "Oh Lord, what shall I say to You and to Mr. Hill on this occasion?" He was about to begin another sentence, when the gentleman interrupted him by observing, "That will do for a beginning.

It is a very excellent first prayer, because it is from the heart. Take the money, and may God's blessing be given along with it." As he spoke, Mr. Hill picked up the two ten-pound notes, transferred them to the half-bewildered man as he cordially shook his hand, and wished him good morning.

It only remains for me to mention that not only did the husband and wife become prosperous in secular matters, but the incident also made so deep an impression on the husband's mind that it ended in his conversion to God [*The Metropolitan Pulpit*, pp. 139-145].

As strange as it was to drive a man to pray, will anyone say it was wrong? My second incident is even wilder, and I give it as I recollect it; if I err in accuracy I apologize, but I will tell it the best as I remember it.

A Methodist preacher went to a certain town in the north, but found hardly anyone to hear him, and he preached for a while with no stir appearing among the dry bones. One Sunday morning he said, "I tell you what it is, friends. This town is responsible to God for the possession of the means of grace that it does not use. I cannot get the people to hear, but I can remove some of their responsibility by destroying the pulpit that they despise, and the place of worship that they will not enter. Here is a start; we will immediately break the desk to pieces, and then if no one comes, we will clear out the pews and everything else, and leave the chapel a wreck. The people will not perish with the gospel so close to them. The candlestick will be taken away since they refuse the light" (cf. Revelation 2:5 KJV). He began by laying his ax at the pulpit, and partly demolishing it before the eyes of the few who were present. "Now," he said, "tell your friends that part of the responsibility is gone, and the rest will follow." The astonished folks went home and spread the amazing news, and before long the place was packed.

You say, "This was an eccentric man." Well, I do not justify his proceedings, but I do judge that he knew better how to handle the situation in his own way than in any way I could have shown him. After all, he was only sacrificing a few boards; and at that small cost he broke through the indifference that more costly methods might have failed to touch. Within a little time Methodism lifted up its head in the town, and the forlorn meetinghouse rang with songs of praise. Why, dear me, if the Metropolitan Tabernacle [see Appendix A, NOTE 3B] was empty, and we were unable to fill the house without doing or saying something astonishing, I think we, too, might run the risk of being thought eccentric, even if it was for the first time in our life.

Everything looks ridiculous, or not, according to its surroundings. Wisdom and wit may become foolishness and even falsehood if they are severed from the occasion that conjured them up. Listen to an ancient tale of a traveler who reported that he had seen a cabbage so large that a whole regiment of soldiers took shelter under it from a rainstorm. To him another, who was no traveler, asked if others would believe him if he told them that on the very day in which this cabbage was seen, he had himself passed by a place where four hundred brass-smiths were making a cauldron – two hundred of them hammering outside, and two hundred inside, fastening the rivets! The traveler eagerly inquired of what use such a cauldron might be, and he received the following answer: "Sir, it was to boil your cabbage." Now, if this second person's story was repeated away from its connection, and its form slightly altered, a richly deserved rebuke would be made to look like an attempt to exceed in lying. Many a word spoken or the principle of answering *a fool according to his folly* (Proverbs 26:4-5) has been quoted against a wise man, and the foolishness has been laid at the wrong door.

There is an extraordinary story of André de Boulanger, a French preacher of great repute, for what was called eccentricity.

He was preaching one afternoon to a congregation of people who disregarded religion both as it pertained to themselves and their families, and he wished simultaneously to convict them and to reprimand them for the bad way in which they were bringing up their little ones. He first asked the children questions from the Catechism, and obtained no replies; he then shook his sleeve, and out flew a deck of cards. The people were shocked by him, of course, but he quietly looked down and said to one of the children, "Boy, bring me a card. You boy, bring me another. You girl, another, and come here with them." They gathered around the pulpit, and he asked one of them, "What is this card, my child?" The boy answered at once. The next, a girl, came up, and she also knew her card. He continued his questions until he had gone through most of the deck, and received correct answers all around. "Ah," he says, "I see how you are training your children. You teach them to know all the cards in a deck, but you do not instruct them in the faith. Are you not ashamed of yourselves?" Here I give no verdict; I could not have done it myself, nor would I like to hear of any friend of mine doing the same, but I cannot judge what was good for Catholics in France so long ago.

Johannes Lassenius, a Dutch court preacher, in the end of the seventeenth century, had been greatly disturbed by seeing a considerable part of his congregation going to sleep. One day he suddenly stopped, and pulling out a battledore [that is, in this case, a small racket used in the game of battledore, a forerunner of badminton] and a shuttlecock, he began playing with them. Of course, the sleepers all woke up directly; the ones most awake jostled their neighbors to share in their astonishment. Then Lassenius turned on them with a severe rebuke. "When I announce to you serious and important truths, you are not ashamed to go to sleep; but when I play the fool, you are all eye and ear." This was sharp medicine for a desperate disease, and the physician who administered it was in terrible danger of injuring himself. I do not think that I can justify this procedure, but I do not know the Dutch people as well as Lassenius did, and my own people never go to sleep, and so I do not pretend to form an opinion one way or the other. Certainly, it must be very provoking to see people sleeping, and yet it is not so very astonishing that they should do so when we consider the drowsy sounds to which they are doomed to listen. "I get so tired of preaching," said a young, bombastic preacher. "Oh man," said a shrewd old listener, "did you say you were tired? If you are only half as tired of it as I am, I pity you." I am afraid that this side of the question is too often forgotten.

The following story is worth mentioning, although I do not hesitate to say that I would have done the same, and would have felt justified, in effect, rebuking an impoverished people for leaving their place of worship in such a shameful condition.

Reverend Zabdiel Adams at one time had an exchange with a neighboring minister – a mild, inoffensive man – who, knowing the peculiar bluntness of his character, said to him, "You will find some panes of glass broken in the pulpit window, and you may possibly suffer from the cold. The cushion, too, is in a bad condition, but I beg of you not to say anything to my people on the subject; they are poor, and sensitive." "Oh no! Oh no!" said Mr. Adams. "You may trust me to be very quiet about such things." But before he left home, he filled a bag with rags and took it with him. When he had been in the pulpit a short time, feeling somewhat inconvenienced by the free circulation of the air, he deliberately took from the bag a handful of rags and stuffed them into the windows. Towards the close of his sermon, which was more or less on the duties of a people towards their minister, he became very animated, and intentionally brought down both fists upon the pulpit cushion with tremendous force. The feathers flew in all directions, and the cushion was nearly emptied. He checked the current of his thoughts, and simply exclaimed, "Why, how these feathers fly!" and then proceeded. He had fulfilled his promise of not addressing the people on the subject, but had taught them a lesson not to be misunderstood. On the next Sunday, the window and cushion were found in excellent repair [*The Book of Clerical Anecdotes*, p. 44].

So far, I have talked to you lightly about eccentric preachers, but I would not have you forget the serious side of the matter. If I was addressing a congregation I would say to them, If you knew how we desire to lay hold of your minds for Christ, and how willingly we would be as solemn as death itself if we thought that this would win your hearts, then you would not so much blame our occasional retorts. If you knew how little we desire notoriety, and how much we desire to save your souls, then you would commend our objective and excuse our style. We ramble because you ramble. Oh, that we could seize the wandering sheep, and bring them home to the true fold. I say, if you knew the desire we have to bring men to Christ, you would not be so eager to go at every little thing that violates the rules of taste. Besides, we are not bound to abide by your judgments. Is it not possible that we know what we are doing just as well as you do? Will you take our work and do it better? If so, we are ready to learn by your example. Judge the preacher if you like, but please do remember that there is something better to be done than that, namely, to get all the good you can out of him, and pray to his Master to put more good into him. What if the man is odd and strange? Yet, as men take pearls out of oyster shells, so may you be willing to accept from God whatever precious truth He sends you. Do not despise the heavenly treasure because of the earthen vessel (cf. 2 Corinthians 4:7 KJV). Do not lose an opportunity of being enriched because the gold lies interconnected with common earth.

And oh, dear brothers, who are engaged in winning souls, let me say to you, by the memories of all these good men who have gone before you, and who were considered eccentric, fear no man's frown, and court no man's smile. Rather, say the right and true thing, and say it the best you can, and ask God's help that you may say it so that you may make men feel it, even though you spur them on to anger, because that man who has discharged his conscience before the living God will be blessed. Do not sacrifice your listeners' souls to save your own reputations. Be fools for Christ's sake, if necessary, so that you may win the unconcerned. The curse of the age is the unearthly ministry that mocks it. I say "unearthly," but I do not mean heavenly; I mean unrealistic, unnatural – a thing that does not hit home in men, or awaken the slightest interest in their minds.

Do you believe that our working class would, as a rule, shun the churches of London if they were entertained there with hearty, simple messages that they could understand, and that would touch their everyday life? I, for one, have reason to speak to the contrary, and to do so without a shadow of a doubt. Do you think that England would be so eager to be enticed back to Rome if all her ministers were preaching the gospel as they should? With such a company of preachers preaching twice every Sunday, besides the weekday exercises, should not our island be illuminated, as by the midday sun, so that it would be impossible for the Roman darkness to return? Things would have been very different if there had been more love, more sincerity, and more passion for souls in the pulpit; but then I greatly fear that there would also have been more eccentric men. Do you dread such evil? I do not share your fear, but instead say, God send it, so that it may be an outgrowth of true life.

Chapter 4

Hugh Latimer

(c. 1487–1555)

Catholic historians have not hesitated to describe Hugh Latimer as extremely eccentric. John Lingard states, "His eloquence was bold and vehement, but poured forth in coarse and sarcastic language, and seasoned with quaint, low jests and buffoonery" [This poor assessment of Latimer comes from the third volume of John Lingard's eight-volume work, *The History of England,* 1806, p. 354]. This accusation is obviously made for the purpose of whitewashing Catholicism and blackening the Reformation. It is with pleasure that we read it, since it prompts us to include the bishop among the noble army of God's slandered servants. We have no wish to deny that Latimer was exceptionally odd, and that flashes of banter often accompanied his earliest sermons and critical debates, but it was always with the view of confounding error and reaching the hearts of his listeners.

Here is an example of his shrewdness. Dr. Buckingham, prior of the Black Friars [see Appendix A, NOTE 4A], endeavored to confute Latimer. In a sermon, he said among other absurd things that the reading of the Scriptures in a common language would cause people to quit their jobs and resort to all types of extremes. "For example," he said, "the plowman, when he hears this in the gospel, *'No one who puts his hand to the plow and looks back is fit for the kingdom of God'* (Luke 9:62), will perhaps stop his plowing. Likewise the baker, when he hears that *a little leaven leavens the whole lump* (Galatians 5:9), may possibly leave our bread unleavened, and our bodies will become malnourished." Latimer heard this sermon, and engaged to answer the arguments. He did so that afternoon, from the same pulpit, with Dr. Buckingham sitting opposite him with his Black Friars' cowl [hood] on his shoulders. After preaching on the figurative phrases of Scripture, Latimer said that such metaphors were commonly used and were well understood in all languages, "as for example," he observed, looking towards the place where the friar sat, "when a painter represents a fox preaching out of a friar's cowl, no one is so feebleminded as to take this for a real fox, but only as a figure of caution to beware of that hypocrisy, deceit, and pretense that lies hidden many times under those cowls."

Latimer's style of preaching – both before and after he became a bishop – was unpretentious and very congenial, perfectly suited to the manners and tastes of his congregation. His sermons should be read by every admirer of plain English. We only have room here for one excerpt that will show how straightforward and colloquial he could be.

"Once, a good man invited one of his friends over for breakfast, and said, 'I hope you can come, but I must tell you ahead of time, you won't have much to eat: one dish, and that's all.' 'What is it?' asked his friend. 'A pudding, and nothing else.' 'Delightful!' said his friend. 'Nothing would make me happier. Of all foods, pudding is my favorite; you may drag me around town with a pudding.' These unscrupulous magistrates and judges follow bribes faster than the fellow would follow the pudding" [*The Third Sermon of M. Hugh Latimer, Preached before King Edward, March twenty-second, 1549* (Romans 15:4); see Select Bibliography].

Latimer wanted his words to be remembered so as to bring about reform, and he did well to put them in such a way that they would ring over the land. We will declare that this pudding story of his did more for the cause of justice than a dozen polished sermons. His was practical preaching, and it dealt with the sins of the great as well as with those of the common people, in tones too honest to be considered polite.

The brazenness of this noble servant of God was seen in his conduct towards King Henry VIII. One New Year's Day, instead of bringing an extravagant gift to the king, as was the custom of that age, Latimer gave him a copy of the New Testament, with a leaf turned down at this passage: *God will judge the sexually immoral and adulterous* (Hebrews 13:4). This might have cost him his life, but Bluff Hal [see Appendix A, NOTE 4B], instead of being angry, admired the good man's courage. On a certain occasion, when preaching before King Henry, Hugh, as was his tendency, spoke his mind very plainly, and the sermon displeased His Majesty; consequently, he was commanded to preach again on the next Sunday, and to apologize for the offense he had given. After reading his text, the bishop began his sermon accordingly: "Hugh Latimer, do you know before whom you are to speak this day? To the high and mighty monarch, the king's most excellent majesty, who can take away your life if you offend; therefore take heed that you speak not a word that may displease! But then consider well, Hugh, do you not know from where you come, on whose message you are sent? Even by the great and mighty God! Who is omnipresent! And who sees all your ways! And who is able to cast your soul into hell! Therefore, take care that you deliver your message faithfully." He then proceeded to preach the same sermon he had preached the preceding Sunday, but with considerably more zeal. The sermon ended, and the king's court was anxious to know what would be the fate of this honest and plain-spoken bishop. After dinner, the king called for Latimer, and with a stern look asked him how he dared preach in such a manner. He, falling on his knees, replied that his duty to his God and his prince had compelled him to speak as he did, and that he had merely accomplished his duty and cleared his conscience by what he had spoken. Upon hearing this, the king, rising from his seat, and taking the good man by the hand, embraced him, saying, "Blessed be God, I have so honest a servant."

Under Edward VI, Latimer enjoyed great influence, but the return of Queen Mary I soon brought him strong opposition. Fearless, honest, and straightforward, Latimer rejoiced when he was called to lay down his bishopric, and when he was summoned to be tried for his life, the old man hastened to appear and defend our holy faith to the death. His words at the stake were typical of the man. Addressing Bishop Nicholas Ridley, who was condemned to die with him, he said, "Be of good comfort, Master Ridley, and play the man. We shall this day light such a candle by God's grace in England as I trust shall never be put out." And by God's grace it never shall be.

Chapter 5

Hugh Peters

(1598–1660)

The most slandered man of his times was Hugh Peters, who was executed at the Restoration [see Appendix A, NOTE 5A] as a ringleader in the so-called Great Rebellion [see Appendix A, NOTE 5B]. He is widely put down as a crude joker, and maligned as a charlatan, although far more evidence indicates that he was a zealous preacher of the gospel. We give him a place here, not because we wholeheartedly admire him, but as a matter of justice to one who has been falsely accused.

In his unconverted life he was an audacious sinner, but after he was converted, he became a powerful preacher of God's Word. At St. Sepulchre's Church [see Appendix A, NOTE 5C] his preaching was very popular; better yet, it was instrumental in the conversion of hundreds. Having implied in a prayer for the queen that she was in need of repentance – as in all probability she was – he was imprisoned by William Laud. Peters ultimately fled England and became a pastor, first in Holland, and then in America. His reputation was so great that his fellow colonists sent him home as a delegate on important business. Here he was detained by the breaking out of the civil wars, during which he became an army chaplain, was present at many great battles, and was frequently sent up to the parliament to report progress.

At one time, Peters was secretary to Oliver Cromwell. Thomas Carlyle quotes his account of the fall of Basing House [see Appendix A, NOTE 5D], and speaks of him as "a man concerning whom the reader has heard so many falsehoods." The Cavaliers exhausted a great amount of animosity in tarnishing this man's reputation to justify his execution by Charles II, when it was nothing more than a political assassination. A respectable biographer [that is, Reverend William Lindsay Alexander; it was he who wrote the entry on Hugh Peters in *The Imperial Dictionary of Universal Biography: A Series of Original Memoirs of Distinguished Men, of All Ages and All Nations, Volume 3* (1863), from which Spurgeon's following citation comes] writes of him, "Peters was not a wise man in all things; he spoke in a blunt and impetuous manner, but he was a true and sincere man – a man of unblemished reputation in circles where nothing foul or mean was tolerated, and a man who in every respect was immensely the superior of those who maligned him" [*The Imperial Dictionary of Universal Biography,* p. 541].

It was commonly expressed in those days that the saints should have the praises of God in their mouths and a two-edged sword in their hands, and this was most often the case with Peters. He was "the fighting parson" of his day; like the ironsides among whom he ministered, he was a devout soldier, and was made a soldier by his devotion. Our views and opinions may run in the opposite direction, but we are too much indebted to the warriors of the Commonwealth to be in a hurry to condemn them. There was an intense earnestness about Hugh Peters, and since his sermons were intended for soldiers, and accustomed to stormy politics, they were in all probability rough-hewn, and by no means pleasant in the ears of Cavaliers; but the inappropriate jokes that were attributed to him were obviously not his, since they were present long before he was born. Some meticulous person has researched and annotated the small volume [that is, a copy of the anonymous compilation titled, *The Tales and Jests of Mr. Hugh Peters* (1660)] in the British Museum that records these awful jokes in such a way as to prove that the majority of the anecdotes are fabrications. [Spurgeon, in the original text, writes, "Some studious owner of the little volume in the British Museum which records these vile witticisms has annotated it in such a way as to prove that the larger number of the anecdotes are fabrications. Thus, 'Jest 1: This is a Norman tale of the twelfth or thirteenth century. Jest 14: Taken from Taylor, the water poet's works,' etc."]

Nevertheless, such stories as the following may have some truth in them.

Praying in a village, Hugh Peters noticed in the church a king of arms, at which point he inserted these words: "Good Lord, keep us from the yoke of tyranny," and spreading his hands towards the king of arms, he said, "Preserve Your servants from the paw of the lion and the horn of the unicorn" [*The Tales and Jests of Mr. Hugh Peters*, p. 41].

Preaching on the advantage Christians have above heathens, and showing that the heathen are guided by a natural instinct, but we Christians have the Word preached to us, he said, "The gospel has a very free passage among us, for I am confident as soon as it enters in at one ear, it goes out at the other" [*The Tales and Jests of Mr. Hugh Peters*, p. 42.]

Mr. Peters, noticing a friend of his, gashed in the head, having been involved in a senseless altercation, began to reprimand him for his indiscretion. "But," he said, "it is too late now to offer advice; come along with me to a surgeon, and I'll see to it that your wound is dressed." Having arrived, the surgeon began to wash away the blood, and search for the man's brains, to see if they were hurt, at which Mr. Peters cries out,

"What a madman you are to look for any such thing; if he had possessed any brains he never would have ventured into such a foolish fight" [*The Tales and Jests of Mr. Hugh Peters,* pp. 34-35].

Hugh Peters sinned against the whole party of Church-and-King by his zealous defense of the parliamentary cause, and at the same time he shocked the Presbyterians by pleading for "a toleration of all sects" – and this was considered the very worst of crimes. Those who are ahead of their times are attacked for principles that eventually become accepted. A man who was secretary to Oliver Cromwell, who had Philip Nye and Thomas Goodwin for close friends, and John Milton for his apologist, was not a bad man – this is morally certain. His peculiarities arose out of his passionate enthusiasm for the cause of liberty, and the extraordinary combination of soldier and preacher in his personality.

In the works of Hugh Peters there are no indications of his being a joker, but there is abundant evidence of his genius and acuity of mind. The little book entitled *A Dying Father's Last Legacy to an Only Child* [see Select Bibliography: Peters, 1683] was written by his own hand just before his execution, and is rich in holy instruction. Here are excerpts:

"He that sets up religion to get anything by it more than the glory of God and the saving his own soul will make a bad bargain of it at the close."

"Make Christ your wisdom. Oh, that you were so wise! Much of wit must be cut off before it will be useful. I have seen the ways of it, although I never could improvise much of it – but this I know, that being unsanctified, wit is a sword in a madman's hand. It spends itself in vanity, foolish joking, and exploitation of those who are weaker than ourselves; yes, it often leads men to play with the blessed Word of God."

"If I go shortly where time shall be no more, where neither rooster nor clock distinguish hours, do not sink, but lay your head in His bosom who can keep you, since He sits on the waves."

Chapter 6

Daniel Burgess

(1645–1713)

The name of Daniel Burgess is usually associated with joking, but this is another instance of the way in which honorable men have been held up to ridicule. He was a Dissenter, and a man of great courage and boldness of speech; he was also a charming and attractive preacher, and so the word was dispatched from the Evil One that he should be denounced as a joker. In those days there was no law to protect the Dissenter, or at least no officer who cared to put it in force, and so Mr. Burgess and his congregation were shamefully harassed by people of the meanest sort; but when he was urged to prosecute these troublemakers, he only replied, "No, I have freely forgiven them, and will never meditate on revenge." These are not the words of a joker.

His listeners leased for him a meetinghouse in Brydges Street, Covent Garden, where a large congregation always gathered. "Being situated," says one of his biographers, "in the neighborhood of the theater, and surrounded by many who were fools enough to mock sin and religion, he frequently had among his listeners those who came only for laughs at the expense of religion, Dissenters, and Daniel Burgess. But his undaunted courage, his pointed wit, and his ready elocution turned this to great advantage. Since he frequently fixed his eye on those scoffers, and addressing them personally in a lively, piercing, and serious manner, he was blessed to see the conversion of many who came only to mock" [The original, preceding text – as reportedly cited from one of Daniel Burgess's biographers – is discoverable only in *History of Dissenters, from the Revolution in 1688, to the Year 1808, Volume 2,* 1809, p. 273, by David Bogue and James Bennett].

He continued as pastor over this congregation for thirty years, during which a new place of worship was built by them in Carey Street, and when this was completely wrecked by Sacheverell's mobs [see Appendix A, NOTE 6A], it was repaired at the expense of the government; but the expense and trouble to which they were put seriously burdened his people. He died on January 26, 1713, at sixty-eight years of age, and was buried at St. Clement Danes, Strand. A writer says [Spurgeon (presumably) derived this anonymous quote from Alexander Chalmers' edition of *The General Biographical Dictionary, Volume 7,* 1813, p. 318], "It has escaped the notice of his biographers, that the celebrated Lord Bolingbroke was once his pupil, and the world has to regret that his lordship did not learn what Daniel Burgess might have taught him; since Daniel, with all his oddities, that made him for so many years the butt of Jonathan Swift, Richard Steele, and the other wits of the time, was a man of real devotion."

One story told of Burgess may possibly have been true, but we are not sure. When expounding on the robe of righteousness (see Isaiah 61:10), he said, "If any of you would have a good and cheap suit, you will go to Monmouth Street; if you want a suit for life, you will go to the Court of Chancery; but if you desire a suit that will last to eternity, you must go to the Lord Jesus Christ, and put on His robe of righteousness." This is probably a garbled quotation. The reader may accept it *cum grano salis* [that is, "with a grain of salt" in Latin, or, "with skepticism"].

Although it pleased the graceless know-it-alls of his day to father silly stories on Burgess, it is clear to all impartial people that he was a man of eminence and of deep devotion. When the Society for the Reformation of Manners [see Appendix A, NOTE 6B] was instituted, he was selected to preach the first sermon. This was published under the title of "The Golden Snuffing," and is a proof of how the good man was vilified. Since a critic describes it as "replete with forced puns," we obtained a copy, but cannot find a pun in it, and barely anything quotable for special uniqueness, unless it is the following passage: "Christ's ministers are your souls' physicians. We are not fiddlers to tickle your ears, nor confectioners to please your palates, but physicians to cure your diseases, and if our most necessary medicines nauseate you, we dare not withhold them and gratify you with sugared poisons." We are sure that the critic never saw the sermon, but judged it from the title alone. The first choice of the preacher by a society that commanded the most capable ministers would not have fallen on a common clown.

Our best evidence that Daniel Burgess was a good and true man is found in the facts that he was thought worthy by his contemporaries to preach one of the sermons in the famous series of "Morning Exercises" [see Appendix A, NOTE 6C], that he was dearly loved by the excellent Dr. William Bates, and that Matthew Henry preached a funeral sermon for him, in which his plainness of speech is fully acknowledged and abundantly justified. Let us conclude our brief notice with an excerpt from this sermon.

He often said he chose rather to be profitable than fashionable in his preaching, and that he thought it cost him more pains to study plainness than it did others to study finesse; and he would be willing to go out of the common way to meet with sinners, to persuade them to return to their God. "That is the best key (he said) that fits the lock, and opens the door, though it is not a silver or a golden one." Many have confessed that they came to hear him at first only to scoff at him and make a joke of what he said, but went away under such convictions about the concerns of their souls and another world, as, it was hoped, ended in a happy change of their spirits.

In his preaching he insisted mostly on the first great principles of religion, in which all good Christians are agreed; and one who was a very competent judge told me that he thought he had as good a faculty in demonstrating them, and making them plain and evident, as most men he ever heard. He greatly lamented and vigorously opposed the growth of deism and infidelity among us, saying he dreaded a "Christless Christianity." He did not meddle with party matters, or matters of doubtful disagreement, but plainly made it his aim to bring people to faith in Jesus Christ, and to live in all godliness and honesty. He was particularly careful to explain the two covenants of works and grace, and to guard against the two rocks of presumption and despair. He now and then used some simple analogies, or surprising turns of expression, or little stories, like those we find in Bishop Hugh Latimer's sermons, that were turned to his reproach by some. But it is certain that many particular stories were maliciously fathered on him that were abominably false, and were raised by a lying spirit only to obstruct his usefulness; and in general, he was industriously misrepresented by many, who it is feared never discovered his proclivity for serious godliness. A gentleman who once went to hear Mr. Burgess out of curiosity, could barely be made to believe that it was him; the man said, "I never heard a better sermon in my life!" [*The Miscellaneous Works of the Rev. Matthew Henry, V.D.M. Volume 2*, 1833, p. 1103].

Chapter 7

John Berridge

(1716–1793)

J ohn Berridge, the vicar of Everton, was commended by John Wesley as one of the most simple as well as most sensible of all whom it pleased God to employ in reviving primitive Christianity. He was a man of remarkable learning, being as familiar in the learned languages as in his native tongue, and well instructed in theology, logic, mathematics, and metaphysics; he was not, therefore, eccentric because he was ignorant. He possessed a strength of understanding, quickness of perception, depth of incisiveness, and brilliancy of imagination beyond most men, while a vein of innocent humor ran through all his public and private discussions. His biographer tells us that this softened what some might call the sternness of religion, and rendered his company pleasant to people of a less serious habit; and yet he adds, "It is very peculiar that it never overcame his own solemnity; he remained serious himself while others were laughing hysterically" [cf. *The Whole Works of the Rev. John Berridge, A.M. Second Edition, with Additions,* 1864, p. xix].

Before he was converted, he preached simple morality, but after he was called by the Holy Spirit, he was zealous for the doctrines of sovereign grace, and preached the gospel in the clearest possible manner. In his ministry he was diligence personified, traveling through the counties of Cambridge, Bedford, Hertford, and Huntingdon continually, preaching on average ten to twelve sermons a week, and riding from place to place on horseback. He wrote to a friend the following:

> I am afraid that my weekly circuits would not suit
> a London or a Bath theologian, nor any delicate
> evangelist that is surrounded with prunella [see
> Appendix A, NOTE 7A]. Long rides and marshy
> roads in severe weather. Cold houses to sit in, with
> very moderate fuel, and three or four children roar-
> ing or rocking around you! Coarse food and meager
> liquor; lumpy beds to lie on that are too short for
> the feet; and stiff blankets like boards for a covering.
> Rise at five in the morning to preach; at seven break-
> fast on tea that smells rancid; at eight mount a horse,
> with boots never cleaned, and then ride home, prais-
> ing God for all mercies [*The Whole Works of the
> Rev. John Berridge,* p. 503; "Letter LXVII. To Lady
> Huntingdon. Everton, Dec. 26, 1767"].

A complaint was brought against him, and the bishop sent for him and reproved him for preaching "at all hours and on all days."

"My lord," he said modestly, "I preach only during two seasons."

"Which are they, Mr. Berridge?"

"In season and out of season, my lord" (cf. 2 Timothy 4:2).

The revival that resulted from his efforts was remarkable for both its depth and duration, and for the personal persecution that it brought on the good man. The clergy and gentry banded together with the vilest mob against him. For twenty to thirty years, "the old devil" was the only name by which he was known, but none of these things moved him. Crowds waited on him wherever he traveled, and his own church was crammed – we would almost say up to the ceiling, since we have heard of men clambering up and sitting on the crossbeams of the roof, while the windows were filled inside and out, and even the outside of the pulpit, to the very top, so that Mr. Berridge seemed almost stifled. There is no wonder that the people swarmed around him, since his style was so intensely plain, simple, and sincere that every plowman was glad to hear the gospel preached in a language that he could understand, and with a sincerity that he could not resist.

His sermons did not follow a set design, and were often mostly improvised. Mr. Berridge says that sometimes while entering the pulpit he found himself unable to manage his thoughts on his subject, and felt himself to be "like a barber's block with a wig on"; but his hearers did not think so, since they were excited to a passionate zeal by his words. On one occasion, while mounting the stairs of the pulpit at Tottenham Court Road, his memory seemed to fail him, and he began his sermon by saying, "I set out to this place tonight with a sack full of fresh-baked wheat bread, that I hoped to set before you, but the bottom came out of the sack as I walked upstairs, and I have nothing left for you but five barley loaves and a few small fishes. You will have those loaves hot from the oven; may they be food convenient for your souls."

His voice was loud, but perfectly controlled; ten or fifteen thousand people frequently made up his congregation in the open air, and he was well heard by all. People came to hear him from twenty miles away, and were at Everton by seven o'clock in the morning, having set out from home soon after midnight. In the early years of his ministry he was the witness of strange scenes, when the revival took the same form as it did a few years ago in certain parts of the north of Ireland [that is, the historic Ulster Revival of 1859], and was accompanied by physical manifestations. The phenomena then presented were very remarkable, but we must confess that we have no faith in their *spiritual* character, and are sorry to hear of their occurrence. After a while the shouting and contortions came to an end, and the work proceeded steadily and after the usual fashion. Amid all the excitement Berridge never lost his head or became a fanatic, neither was he exalted above measure, but remained one of the humblest and most genuine of men.

There is no doubt that his style was very remarkable, and entirely his own. In one of his letters he writes,

> I have been recruiting for Henry Venn at Godmanchester, a thickly populated and wicked town near Huntingdon, and was greeted with a patient reception from a large audience. I hope he also will set aside a few barns, and preach in them to fill up his fold at Yelling; surely, reason exists when souls are perishing for lack of knowledge. Must salvation give place to imaginary etiquette, and sinners go flocking to hell through our dread of unconventionality? While unconventionality in its worst shape roams the kingdom with impunity, should not unconventionality in its best shape pass without censure? I told my brother he has no need to fear being slandered for sheep-stealing while he only whistles the sheep to a better pasture, and messes neither with the flesh nor the fleece; and I am sure he cannot sink much lower in reputation, since he has lost his character uprightly

by preaching the gospel without butchering it.
The scoffing world makes no other distinction
between us than between Satan and Beelzebub; we
both have tufted horns and cloven feet, only I am
thought the more impudent devil of the two. [*The
Whole Works of the Rev. John Berridge,* pp. 384-
385; "Letter XIV. To John Thornton, Esq. Everton,
Aug. 10, 1774"]

Berridge cared little if the wicked world treated him as it did
his Master; he only longed to save those who loved to condemn
him. His works are published in an accessible form [see Select
Bibliography: *The Whole Works of the Rev. John Berridge,
A.M. Second Edition, with Additions*], and all that we know
of his life will be found in the memoir [by Reverend Richard
Whittingham] that precedes them; there is consequently no
reason for us to enlarge further.

Chapter 8

Rowland Hill

(1745–1833)

I t is not our intention to write a life of Rowland Hill, but only to sketch an outline portrait from the *eccentric* point of view. As a preacher, Mr. Hill was the child of John Berridge, whose church he attended while he was a student at Cambridge, riding over to Everton every Sunday to hear him. From that veteran he no doubt learned the freedom and simplicity of language that always distinguished him. He also associated a lot with John Stittle, one of Berridge's converts, and a man of distinct individuality, who preached in Green Street, Cambridge, for many years. The degree of intimacy between the two men may be gathered from the incident recorded by William Jones [in his *Memoir of the Rev. Rowland Hill, M.A. Third Edition,* 1845]:

> On one occasion, when Rowland Hill was on his
> way to Duxford, to preach for the Missionary
> Society, he suddenly exclaimed, "I must go to
> Cambridge, and see the widow of an old minister,

who lives there, because I have a message to give her." He was urged not to go, but held firm to his purpose. He spent a short time with the respectable widow, and reached Duxford just before the evening service. On entering his friend's (Mr. Payne's) house he said, "Dear me, I forgot to give my message to the widow," and seemed almost determined to return to Cambridge. But he stayed for the service, and when asked whether the message he had forgotten was important, he replied, "Yes sir; I wanted the old lady, who will soon be in heaven, to give my love to Johnny Stittle, and tell him I will see him again soon." [*Memoir of the Rev. Rowland Hill, M.A. Third Edition*, pp. 62-63]

Mr. Hill's first opportunities to preach were of an itinerant nature. He was glad to preach at a large church, and equally delighted to preach at a small meetinghouse; but if the village green, a barn, a lecture hall, or a shack were offered, he would preach at these just the same. He was not raised in the lap of luxury as a preacher, nor was he surrounded by the society of aloof aristocracy, so as to be guarded from every whiff of the air of common life. He mingled so thoroughly with the people that he became the people's man, and forever remained so. With all the bold confidence that should go with nobility he combined with an unassuming simplicity and benevolence of spirit that made him dear to people of all ranks. He was thoroughly a man, thinking and acting for himself with all the freedom of a great emancipated mind, that bowed only at the feet of Jesus; but he was essentially a man-child, a Nathanael *in whom there [was] no deceit!* (John 1:47) – uninhibited, natural, transparent, in all things unassuming, and true. He once said of a man who knew the gospel but seemed afraid to preach it, "He preaches the truth as a donkey munches a thistle – very cautiously." This was exactly the opposite of his own way of doing it.

His set places of ministry were Surrey Chapel and Wotton-under-Edge. He facetiously called himself "Rector of Surrey Chapel, Vicar of Wotton, and Curate of all the fields and lanes throughout England and Wales." Surrey Chapel was called by many "the Round-house," and it was reported that its shape was chosen by Mr. Hill so that the devil might not have a corner to hide in. The neighborhood is described by John Berridge "as one of the worst spots in London, the very paradise of demons." It was right by the assembling ground of Lord George Gordon's Protestant rowdies [see Appendix A, NOTE 8A], and was in many respects an unsavory spot, and therefore so much the more in need of the gospel. The spacious structure was the center of philanthropic, educational, and religious work of all kinds, and it would be difficult to find a building from which more beneficial influences have emanated.

At Wotton, Mr. Hill lived in what he called "a paradisiacal spot," having his house near the chapel, and lovely scenery all around. He says of the village, "This place, when I first came to Gloucestershire, was filled with brutal persecutors; but now, since they have been blessed with the gospel, they have been wonderfully softened." We visited the place with great interest, and were taken to the spot where dear old Rowland would sit with his telescope and watch the people coming down the neighboring hills to the meeting, and would afterwards astonish them by mentioning what he had seen. Both in London and in the country he was the universal benefactor, and he mixed with all sorts of people. In London he might be seen in the streets with his hands behind him, gazing into the shop windows, and in the country the cottages and the cornfields were his study. A friend told me an anecdote that I have never come across in print. When at Wotton, Rowland Hill heard of a woman who was well-known for her sausages, and so he went to her place and bought a supply. "Now, my good woman," he said, "how is it that you make such good sausages?" "Why sir," she said, "I think it is a gift from the Almighty." Mr. Hill shook his head at this, and began to repent of his bargain – as well he should – since the articles turned out to be stale. He later told the story to illustrate how people try to pass off their bad goods with big talk, and as a proof of the fact that fanaticism is often in alliance with trickery, he said, "A gift from the Almighty! And yet that which this precious gift makes is good for nothing." We give this as an instance of the manner in which he turned every little incident into a good illustration.

Our friend Vernon J. Charlesworth, headmaster of the Stockwell Orphanage, has written a life of Rowland Hill [see Select Bibliography: Charlesworth, *Rowland Hill; His Life, Anecdotes, and Pulpit Sayings,* 1876; also see Appendix A, NOTE 8B], that in our opinion surpasses its predecessors in giving a full-length portrait of the good man, and as this is readily available in print, we refer our readers to it. We remember reading an article in one of the reviews of the day in which Mr. Hill was abused after the manner of *The Saturday* [see Appendix A, NOTE 8C]. It gave us great comfort to see how those who came before us endured the tongue of malice and survived its venom. It is clear from many remarks made by contemporary writers, and especially from the way in which one of his biographers has tried to take the very soul out of him by toning down his wit, that he was regarded by many serious people as a good brother whose imperfections were to be endured but also quietly censured. Now, we are not at all of this mind. Rowland Hill may have been too liberal with his use of humor, perhaps, but this was better than smothering it and all his other faculties, as many do, beneath a huge feather bed of stupid propriety.

When we hear our long-faced brothers condemning all joy,

we remember the story of holy Dr. James Durham, the Scottish preacher who wrote a commentary on the Song of Solomon, and another on the book of Revelation. His biographers say of him that he was so serious at all times that he very seldom smiled, much less laughed, at anything. We wonder if he had any children. If so, what kind of father must he have been? But here is the story in the old-fashioned language in which we find it. Reverend Mr. William Guthrie, minister at Finwick, met with Mr. Durham at a gentleman's house near Glasgow, some time before his last sickness, and observing that he was in a somewhat somber mood, attempted to make him smile and laugh, by his facetious and lighthearted conversation. Mr. Durham was rather disgusted and displeased at Mr. Guthrie's innocent display of frivolity. When Mr. Guthrie, according to the honorable custom of that family, and at their request, prayed, he showed the utmost seriousness, composure, and devout liveliness. When he rose from prayer, Mr. Durham tenderly embraced his friend, and said to him, "Oh William, you are such a happy man. If I had been as happy as you were before you went to pray, I would not have been in a frame of mind for prayer, or any other religious exercises for two days." This occurrence led Mr. Durham to be more lenient in his judgment of his lively brothers, and our trust is that it may have a similar effect on any sour person who may happen to read this little book.

Rowland Hill's name is very sweet in South London, and if you happen to meet with one of his old listeners, it will do your heart good to see how their eyes will sparkle at the mere mention of his name. He made religion a delight, and the worship of God a pleasure; yes, he made just the memory of it to be a joy forever to the hearts of the aged as they recalled the days of their youth when Rowland Hill – dear old Rowland Hill as they liked to call him – was in his glory.

Chapter 9

Matthew Wilks

(1746–1829)

What Rowland Hill was on one side of the River Thames, Matthew Wilks was on the other. He came to London in 1775, and John Berridge took part in his ordination over the Tabernacle churches that had been unified by George Whitefield. He was a person of commanding appearance, of great shrewdness, and of unique individuality, and, like other worthy men, he has been much distained because a vein of humor was evident in him. This matters little, since the good man led multitudes to Jesus, and was a faithful pastor to the flock that he led. He was one of the fathers of the London Missionary Society, *The Evangelical Magazine,* the Irish Evangelical Society, the Bible Society, and the Religious Tract Society; in fact, from his great practical wisdom, he was called on to be a leader in all kinds of Christian work.

Many an odd phrase has fallen from his lips. For instance, when he wished to explain the text, *Look carefully then how you walk* (Ephesians 5:15), he pictured a cat walking on the top of a high wall covered with bits of broken glass bottles. We have heard this illustration quoted with ridicule, but we fail to see any objection to it. Let anyone watch a cat in such circumstances, and then find a better instance of *careful walking* if he can. We do not believe the traditional idea that he rebuked the headdresses of the day by preaching on "top [k]not go down," which is a clipping from the text, *Let the one who is on the housetop not go down* (Matthew 24:17); but we have met a gentleman who said that he saw him hold up a small pair of scales when preaching from the verse that says, *"You have been weighed in the balances"* (Daniel 5:27). We do not wish to doubt our informant, but we think it is probable that no actual scales were present, but that Wilks simply imitated the holding up of balances and the act of weighing that in later years the memory became a little aided by the imagination, and actual scales and weights were furnished in the narrator's mind.

Mr. Wilks's anniversary sermon for the London Missionary Society was an extraordinary one. Certainly the text was remarkable enough. *The children gather wood, the fathers kindle fire, and the women knead dough, to make cakes for the queen of heaven. And they pour out drink offerings to other gods, to provoke me to anger* (Jeremiah 7:18).

When the text was announced, in the midst of a crowded assembly, every eye seemed to express astonishment at the preacher's choice. He had not proceeded far, however, in his undertaking, when the feeling of astonishment gave way to pure delight, when all seemed convinced that though the text was uncommon, it was by no means inappropriate. Having glanced at the idolatrous worship of the queen of heaven, the zeal of the worshippers, and the people employed in it, he then said, "I will *contrast* your objects, *compare* your zeal, and *muster* your agents." The appeal was admirably directed, and energetically sustained, and from the hearing and perusal of that part of it that referred to the agents (namely, *the children, the fathers, and the women*) arose the system of auxiliary institutions that now pervades the whole country, and combines in its support young and old, rich and poor. Perhaps seldom has such an extraordinary effect sprung from the preaching of a single sermon. Irrespective, however, of its impression as delivered from the pulpit, it possesses considerable merit, as an argument and as a composition. [That which is believed to be the original article – as discovered in *The Evangelical Magazine and Missionary Chronicle 1829*, p. 134 – from which Spurgeon quotes anonymously, he adds that Wilks's sermon was "preached before the Missionary Society, at Surrey Chapel, in the month of May, 1812, which, if not the most eloquent, was, beyond all dispute, the most ingenious, and, we might add with safety, the most effective sermon ever preached before that Society."]

Beyond a pitiful little memoir and a few basic sermon outlines, nothing remains of all the great and good things that were spoken by Mr. Wilks, and the stories told of him relate to him as a man rather than as a preacher. My esteemed friend Mr. George Rogers has given me the following note:

"Matthew Wilks was very comical in his appearance, in his voice, and in his language. Like Rowland Hill, he was sound in his gospel views, was very practical, and deservedly popular. He has called on me, and frequently asked that I preach for him at 'both tabs' [see Appendix A, NOTE 9A] as he called them. He had a serious side, but a tender heart. I will make mention of two incidents that I received from a mutual friend of Mr. Wilks and I, and that I believe to be authentic. When John Williams was recommended to the London Missionary Society, and nearly all the directors were against him, he found a determined supporter in Mr. Wilks, who even went so far in pressing the point as to be charged with being overbearing. When the debate was over, Mr. Wilks went into the room where

Mr. Williams was waiting for the decision of the committee and said, 'Well, young man, you have been accepted, but if it had not been for my overbearing disposition you would have never gotten in.'" This was Williams the martyr at Erromango [see Appendix A, NOTE 9B].

A minister from the West of England having called on Mr. Wilks, informed him that he was in great mental distress on account of debt. Mr. Wilks said, "You are a great fool; you should not get in debt."

"Oh," he replied, "but it accumulated gradually, and I could not help it. My wife was ill, and some of my children died, and my income is extremely small."

"How much do you owe?"

"About £70" [70 British pounds].

"Then you are a great fool. I want you to preach at Greenwich next Sunday."

"Oh, I am awfully depressed."

"But I insist that you must go, and I will send a note to the gentleman with whom you must dine."

Returning to Mr. Wilks on Monday morning, he told him the gentleman with whom he dined gave him £10. "Well," said Mr. Wilks, "but you are a fool for getting into debt for all that." He then produced another £10, and said he had obtained that from another gentleman for him. Observing him to be greatly affected by this, Mr. Wilks added, "Still you are a great fool." He then produced another £10, called him a fool more vehemently than before, and continued to put £10 before him again and again, and to scold him until the whole £70 was produced; and then he said, "Now go home, and don't be such a fool as to get into debt again." This showed a great knowledge of human nature, since he consequently kept the good man from being overwhelmed by the great and unexpected relief.

But Mr. Wilks could be fearfully harsh, and when he had

doubts about the ability or character of a candidate for the ministry, he showed no mercy. On one occasion he had badgered
and browbeaten a young man to such a degree that he was barely
able to answer a single question. "Man," said Mr. Wilks, "you'll
never be fit for the ministry; you seem to know nothing at all.
Can you tell the difference between me and Moses?" "Nonsense,
Mr. Wilks," intervened good Dr. Alexander Waugh, anxious to
release the young victim. "You should not ask the boy a question
like that; but if you please, I will tell you the difference between
Moses and you: Moses was the meekest of men."

His manner of finding a wife for a fellow minister was more
genial. He sent him to the lady's house with this short note:

"My dear madam, allow me to introduce to you my
worthy friend, Reverend Mr. A ——.
"If you're a cat
"You'll smell a rat!
"Yours truly,
"Matt Wilks."

The lady found it necessary to request the gentleman to explain
the letter; this led them into pleasant conversation, and into
mutual admiration that ended in marriage. As a result, the mys-
tery of the cat and the rat was solved [see Select Bibliography:
Grant, 1839, pp. 82-83].

We may not imitate his facetiousness, but it would be a
happy circumstance if all ministers read the Bible as diligently
as he did, since he read it carefully through four times in the
year. He was careful that his associate pastors and assistants
were well remunerated, but he would only receive £200 a year
himself, and of that he gave £100 away. He loved the poor, and
his poor people loved him. His power over his members was
very great, because it was founded in love. The common people gladly listened to him, and he enjoyed a long and fruitful
ministry among them. The works that he initiated have been

perpetuated, especially the societies that he helped to establish. The Lord, as a result, has enabled his work to endure the fiery ordeal of time, which is a severe test, causing many grandiose ministries to pass away as smoke. Call him eccentric if you like, but our prayer shall be to the Lord that we may share in the blessing that rests on the labors of Matthew Wilks. *Establish the work of our hands upon us; yes, establish the work of our hands!* (Psalm 90:17).

Chapter 10

William Dawson

(1773–1841)

Wiilliam Dawson, the Yorkshire farmer and Methodist preacher, should be mentioned among the eccentrics, but not on account of any great use of humor in his preaching. Barefaced lies were fabricated concerning him, and he was made out to look like a mere comedic actor by the secular world, but there was nothing about his preaching to deserve it. He was gifted at retort, and there was a slight mixture of whimsy in his sermons, but he was mainly distinguished for his wonderful dramatic power, by which he made everything stand out before the people's eyes, and created the most profound impressions.

In a note from Dr. George Osborn to us, that gentleman says, "Humor was not Dawson's specialty; it was the intense activity and fervor of his imagination, with a basis of sound doctrine and sound character, that was the source of his power, and a mighty power it was."

In a brief sketch of Mr. Dawson, by R. A. West, we read the following description of his outer man, that lets us see the farmer and the preacher combined:

I first heard Mr. Dawson from the pulpit in the
year 1828. His apparel and demeanor struck me as
unclerical. True, he wore a black coat and vest, and
a white neckcloth, but his lower extremities were
encased in a pair of drab pants, and he wore what
are technically called 'top boots' that were at the
time universally worn in England by subsistence
farmers as a part of their Sunday or market-day
attire. He crossed the floor of the chapel on his
way to the pulpit with a rolling gait, as though he
were walking a plowed field, with a hand in each
pants pocket, half whistling, half humming the air
of a good old Methodist tune. He was apparently
unconscious of this, since his eyes were turned
downward in a trance, and he seemed cut off from
all surrounding objects. In all my subsequent
knowledge of him I never saw a repetition of the
mood. [R. A. West's preface to the book, *Sermons
by the Late Mr. William Dawson, of Barnbow near
Leeds,* 1860, pp. vi-vii]

He was always natural and farmerlike; the smell of a divinely
blessed field was on him, and the multitude delighted to hear
him. His power in setting an illustration before his listeners
will be seen from the following:

Preaching on the returning prodigal
(Luke 15:11-32), Mr. Dawson paused, looked at the
door, and shouted out, after he had depicted him
in his wretchedness, "There he comes, slipshod!
Make way – make way – make way there." Such
was the approach to reality, that a considerable
part of the congregation turned to the door, some

rising on their feet, under the momentary impression that someone was entering the chapel in the state described. In the same sermon, paraphrasing the father's response to his angry son who would not go in, he said, "Do not be offended; surely a calf may do for a prodigal, shoes for a prodigal, a ring and a robe for a prodigal, but *all that is mine is yours*" (Luke 15:31). As to the more brilliant display, when pointing to the door, similar results were produced when referring to the witch of Endor (1 Samuel 28). His illustration took such hold on the imagination, that on exclaiming, "Wait – Wait! There she is!" some of the poor people inadvertently directed their eyes downward, where his own eye was fixed, and the spot to which he was pointing, as if she were about to rise from beneath their feet, and become visible to the congregation.

The next excerpt is part of the closing remarks of Dawson's sermon, "Death on the Pale Horse" from Revelation 6:7-8. *When he opened the fourth seal, I heard the voice of the fourth living creature say, "Come!"* (Revelation 6:7ff).

"'Come and see,' then, the awful condition of an unsaved sinner. Open your eyes, sinner, and see it for yourself. There he is in the broad road of ruin; every step he takes is deeper in sin; every breath he draws feeds his corruption; every moment takes him farther from heaven and closer to hell. Onward, onward he is going – death and hell are after him; they quickly and untiringly pursue him – with swift but noiseless hoof the pale horse and his pale rider are tracking the godless wretch. See! See! They are getting closer; they are overtaking him." At this moment the stillness of the congregation was so complete that the ticking of the clock could be distinctly heard in every part of the chapel. On this, with a flair peculiarly his own, he promptly seized the moment, without the slightest interruption. Leaning over the pulpit with an attitude of intense scrutiny, and fixing his keen eye on those who sat right in front of him, he continued in an almost supernatural whisper. "Listen! Listen! That swift rider is coming, and judgment is following him. That is his untiring footstep! Listen!" And then imitating for a moment or two the beat of the pendulum, he exclaimed in the highest pitch of his voice, "Lord, save the sinner! Save him! Death is upon him, and hell follows! See, the long arm is raised! The final arrow is aimed! Oh my God, save him, save him, because if the rider overtakes that poor sinner, unpardoned and unsaved, and strikes his blow, down he falls, and backward he drops – hell behind him, and as he falls backward, he looks upward, and shrieks, 'Lost! Lost! Lost! Time lost; Sundays lost; means lost; soul lost; heaven lost! All lost, and lost forever!' Backward he drops; all his sins seem to hang around his neck like countless millstones as he plunges into the burning abyss. 'Come and see.' Lord, save him! Oh my God, save him! 'Come and see.' Blessed be God! The rider has not overtaken him yet; there is still time and space for that poor sinner, he may yet be saved – he has not dropped into hell. 'Come and see.' The horse and the rider have not overtaken you yet; there is, therefore, an 'accepted time,' there is a 'day of salvation'! 'Come and see.' There is God the Father inviting you; God the Father commanding you; God the Father swearing He has no pleasure in your death, but in your life. There is Jesus Christ; He has come to seek you. He has traveled thirty years to save you. He is dying on the cross. With His outstretched arms He says, 'Come to Me, and I will give you rest; He who believes in Me shall never die!'" (cf. Matthew 11:28 and John 11:).

The effect was so overwhelming that two of the congregation

fainted, and it required all the preacher's tact and self-control to ride through the storm that his own vivid imagination had aroused [cf. *Sermons by the Late Mr. William Dawson, of Barnbow near Leeds,* pp. 27-43].

Those must have been moving services where his listeners responded audibly to his appeals. On one occasion when he exhorted his listeners to give their hearts to the Lord, he added, with his hand on his chest and his eyes towards heaven, "Here's mine." A voice from the gallery called out, "Here's mine, too, Billy!"

Preaching at Ancoats, Manchester, on Judges 8:4 – *"Exhausted yet pursuing"* – every eye all at once seemed covered with tears; and when people and preacher were elevated to the highest pitch of feeling, a momentary pause took place, during which the clock struck twelve and broke the silence that reigned, like the hammer on the bell at a watch night, on the departure of the old year. In an instant his eyes darted to the front of the gallery, and personifying the timepiece, he said, "You may speak, clock, but I am not done yet." Though no apparent expectation existed on the part of his listeners that he would finish his sermon with the hour, yet it had all the effect of reviving disappointed hope, and threw a gleam of sunshine onto every face.

William Dawson was a man by himself. When God formed him, He broke the mold, but we wish He had given us at least one more like him in manner and discipline. Of his power in witty answers we will only give one example, and then close our note. The following dialogue occurred between Dawson and a faultfinding gentleman.

Gentleman: "I had the pleasure of hearing you preach yesterday."

Mr. Dawson: "I hope you not only heard but also profited."

Gentleman: "Yes, I did, but I don't like those prayer meetings at the end. They destroy all the goodness previously received."

Mr. Dawson: "You should have united with the people in them."

Gentleman: "I went into the gallery, where I hung over the front, and saw the whole crowd, but got nothing out of the experience. To be honest, I lost all the benefits I had received during your sermon."

Mr. Dawson: "It is easy to account for that."

Gentleman: "How so?"

Mr. Dawson: "You climbed to the top of the house, and as you were looking down your neighbor's chimney to see what kind of a fire he kept, you got your eyes filled with smoke. If you had entered by the door, and gone into the room, and mingled with the family around the household hearth, you would have enjoyed the benefit of the fire just as they did. Sir, you have got the smoke in your eyes."

Chapter 11

Jacob Gruber

(1778–1850)

When the population of the United States was sparse and widely scattered, public religious services could not have been maintained at all if the Lord had not raised up a zealous race of itinerant preachers, who passed rapidly from one hamlet or homestead to another, and by their intense earnestness kept alive the sacred fire. We allude to a period ranging from the late eighteenth century to the mid nineteenth century. The men of that time were physically strong out of necessity, or they would not have endured the hardships of their roving mission, and they were also sturdy mentally, and needed to be so, since they dealt with people who required vigorous handling. Of course they were rough and unrefined – what could they have accomplished if they had been otherwise? Of what use would a razor be in clearing a forest? Quite often they were wildly humorous as well as impetuously zealous, but this play of their spirits was probably necessary to keep them from sinking down under the burdens of their uncomfortable and trying circumstances. At any rate, they did the work that God gave them to do, and left America a Christian country instead of a pagan one, which it might very well have become had it not been for their efforts. We do not commend everything that they did, much less hold them up for imitation; but we think it is profitable to see how others performed their work, and as a result we will describe Jacob Gruber, of whom his contemporaries said, "He is a character, and copies no man." We will do little more than give extracts from a biography written by W. P. Strickland [The biography from which Spurgeon gleans much of this chapter's information is W. P. Strickland's *The Life of Jacob Gruber* (1860)], that has not been published in England. We will make a long chapter of this, because we will regard Gruber as a sort of specimen of the backwoods American evangelist.

At the beginning of the nineteenth century there appeared at the seat of the Philadelphia Conference [that is, the first annual conference of (American) Methodists, held in Philadelphia, 1800] a young man who was impressed with the conviction that it was his duty to preach. His parents were of German descent, and had been brought up in the faith of the great leader of the Reformation, Martin Luther. The German Reformed Church [see Appendix A, NOTE 11A] for many years had the exclusive control of the religious interests of the neighborhood. The time came, however, when this calm was broken. Two itinerant Methodist preachers had divided up the country into circuits, and, claiming to be successors of the apostles, thought it proper to imitate them in traveling across the country, and preaching the gospel wherever they found an open door. The strangeness of their manner, and the wonderful sincerity of their preaching, attracted the attention of the people, particularly the younger generation; the cabins and barns where they held their meetings were crowded.

Young Gruber listened to these circuit preachers with

amazement. Though they were denounced by the prim and proper Reformers as wild and fanatical, he nevertheless felt strangely drawn to their meetings. There was such an intense passion in their prayers, such a zeal and earnestness in their preaching, and such a power in their songs, that he was entirely fascinated, and soon became convinced of his need for conversion. His prayers for a change of heart were soon answered, and with gladness he went with his parents to the place of meeting, and with them joined the Methodist church [*The Life of Jacob Gruber,* pp. 9-11].

So that the reader may have a correct description of the spiritual condition of this particular neighborhood, we give an account prepared by Gruber himself. He says, "The Methodist preachers came into the neighborhood and held several meetings. As the result of their labors a revival commenced, and quite a few people were converted and professed a knowledge of sins forgiven." Some of the members of the German minister's church went to the old gentleman, expressing a desire to know something about this new doctrine. In reply to their inquiries about the knowledge of forgiveness, he said, "I have been a preacher for more than twenty years, and I do not know my sins are forgiven, and indeed it is impossible that anyone should know it." It came as no surprise to some that this preacher was in darkness on that subject, since he frequently became intoxicated. An elderly woman – a member of the German church – at one of the revival meetings where some were praising God for having pardoned their sins, stood thoughtfully shaking her head and said, "It cannot be; if they had to answer a hundred and sixty questions, as I had to before I got religion, they would learn that it is impossible to obtain forgiveness so quickly."

Among the early itinerant preachers who visited Pennsylvania around this time was the eccentric Valentine Cook. He was fresh from the halls of Cokesbury College, and perhaps the first native college-bred preacher that had appeared in the American Methodist Church. When Cook made his appearance, and it was rumored that he was a college graduate, he attracted widespread attention. The German Reformed Church, like several other churches we might name, entertained the idea that it was impossible for a man who had not received a formal education to be qualified to preach; and because of that, vastly more respect was paid to Cook than to any of his colleagues in the ministry. His learning, however, did not always avail to guarantee him respect, as the following incident will show.

"After traveling a whole day without refreshment in a region where he was unknown, he halted in the evening at the house of a German, and asked if he could obtain some feed for his horse and something for himself to eat. Being a tall, rough-looking specimen of humanity, the good woman, who was busy spinning yarn, took him to be an Irishman. She was not at all favorably impressed with his appearance, but at her husband's request she fixed a lunch for him and returned to her spinning wheel, saying to her husband somewhat irritably in German, that she hoped the Irishman would choke while eating. After Cook had finished his meal, he asked for the privilege to pray, which being granted he knelt down and offered up a fervent petition in German. In his prayer he asked the Lord to bless the kind woman at the wheel and give her a new heart, so that she might be more hospitable towards strangers. Such a personal reflection was more than the good woman could stand, and she left her spinning wheel and ran from the house overwhelmed with chagrin at her wicked wish."

We mention these incidents for the purpose of giving the reader some idea of the times in which young Gruber began his religious career. Being a sprightly lad, he was soon called out to exercise his gifts in public prayer and exhortation. As usual in these cases, a storm of persecution arose, not only from those who were outside the church and family, but also from his own household. Father, mother, brothers, and sisters, as if by one consent, rose up against the young exhorter, and he was forced to leave home and seek more congenial quarters elsewhere. Some of the more zealous Methodists interpreted this differently from what young Jacob had imagined, and persuaded him that it was a clear indication of Providence – that it was his duty to abandon everything for the exclusive work of the ministry. This interpretation of Providence was soon afterwards verified. As he went his way alone and on foot to the town of Lancaster, he met one of the itinerant preachers, who in a short conversation convinced him of the duty of entering the ministry, and sent him to an adjoining circuit to fill a vacancy. He accordingly procured a horse and went to the appointment [*The Life of Jacob Gruber*, pp. 13-16].

As the conference embraced sickly regions in its territory, he never did know when the fearless Bishop Francis Asbury might send him to one of these locations, if for no other reason than to test his courage. While many young men had failed in their course, having given up after only a year's service, this was not to be the case with Gruber. He had a powerful constitution, and an iron frame capable of enduring an amount of hardship, labor, and fatigue that made him the wonder of all his ministerial companions.

The second year of our young, itinerant preacher's ministry was spent where vast tracts of wilderness intervened between the appointments, and new hardships were to be endured. Dauntless, he scaled the mountains, infiltrated the woods, and sought the cabins nestling among them, so that he might preach the gospel to their inhabitants. Here he labored with the most unremitting zeal and diligence. Through his fervent appeals many were awakened and converted.

At a certain place on this circuit there lived a man who had been in great distress of mind, bordering on despair. He wept a lot and prayed almost constantly, but found no relief. Gruber visited him and talked with him for a considerable amount of time, quoting Bible passages that were applicable to his case. The man could not, however, be persuaded that any promise was for him; he believed his day of mercy and hope was gone forever. The following conversation then took place between Gruber and the despairing man:

"What will become of you?" Gruber asked him.

"I shall be lost," he answered.

"Where will you go?"

"To hell."

"But if you go there, you will have it all to yourself."

"What do you mean?"

"I mean just what I say: if you go to hell weeping and praying, you will scare all the devils away, because I have never heard or read of one going to hell weeping and praying." At this a smile came over the man's face like sunshine on a cloud; his despair was gone, and hope full and joyous sprang up in his soul [*The Life of Jacob Gruber,* pp. 25-26].

At the next conference Gruber was sent to the Winchester circuit, partnered with a young male colleague by the name of Richards. This young, itinerant preacher greatly annulled his usefulness by getting the notion into his head that, to maintain ministerial dignity, he had to put on extra airs of reserve and sanctity. A *sad countenance,* as our old English version has it, in the description of the Pharisees in the days of the Savior [an allusion to Matthew 6:16 KJV: *Moreover when ye fast, be not, as the hypocrites, of a sad countenance: for they disfigure their faces, that they may appear unto men to fast. Verily I say unto you, They have their reward*], is not a true indication of spirituality. One of the old preachers who had outlived his day, and was constantly harping on one string, "You are fallen! You are fallen!" remarked on a certain occasion that he wished some of the old preachers were as solemn as that young man. Bishop Asbury, who was present when this remark was made, smilingly said, "Do you make any allowance for solids and fluids?" [that is, flesh and blood]. We recollect a reply once made by a lighthearted, joyous, talented young preacher to a devout lady, who said to him in a reproving manner, "I wish you would be as serious as Brother C." "Ah!" said the young brother, laughingly, "when I get indigestion as bad as he has it, I will, no doubt, be equally serious" [*The Life of Jacob Gruber*, pp. 30-31].

He had now been six years in the work of the ministry, and had exhibited such good proof of his faithful calling and success that the good Bishop Asbury deemed him qualified for the more responsible post of presiding elder, and accordingly, in the year 1807, he was appointed to the presidency of Greenbrier district. It embraced a wild region of country in Virginia, said to be the roughest in the bounds of the Baltimore Conference. To use his own language, he had "hard work, rough fare, and bad roads"; but by way of offset to these disadvantages he had "great meetings." Towards the close of the year, camp meetings were held on every circuit, and hundreds were converted. Indeed, a camp meeting in those days without numerous conversions and large admissions to the church would have been a great wonder.

At that time even a quarterly meeting was considered dull and profitless unless souls were converted and added to the church, and a revival was inaugurated for the coming quarter. In describing these camp meetings, Gruber said, "Some complained about too much wildfire, and called the preachers the fire company; but we wanted fire that would warm and melt, not tamed fire, fox fire, and the like." During the three years in this district he experienced many hardships. In describing his labors he says, "One very cold winter night I took a path as a shortcut to my stopping place, but got out of my course, wandered about among the hills and mountains, and went to the top of one of them to see clearings, or hear dogs bark, or roosters crow, but all in vain. After midnight the moon arose; I could then see my track. The snow was knee-deep, and I went back until I got onto the right course, and reached my lodging between four and five o'clock in the morning. The family was alarmed, and said I was late, but I called it early. After lying down and sleeping a little I woke up, ate breakfast, and then departed on my day's journey, filling two appointments."

At the end of his first year in the district he had a line of appointments reaching to Baltimore. On his route he passed through a wild, mountainous region, journeyed over by a remote path. Not a single cabin was to be found within a distance of twenty miles. He hit the trail on the mountain at about ten o'clock, but had not gone many miles before he found it covered up knee-deep in snow, and not a single track was to be seen. He picked his way, however, as best he could, and traveled on. During the day it began to rain, which rendered his journey even more uncomfortable. At length he reached Cheat River, and found it considerably swollen, with ice in the middle. When he reached the ice, he reluctantly dismounted, and then making his horse leap upon it he again mounted. The ice did not break, and he was able to reach the other shore. He traveled on in the woods until night overtook him, when he lost his path and became entangled in the forest. The rain that had been pouring down now changed into snow, and the wind blew furiously. Besides all this, it was becoming increasingly cold. He did not know what to do, except pray. The night was spent sitting on his horse. Above the roar of the storm he could hear the scream of the mountain lion and the howl of the wolf. It was a dreadful night; but morning came, and with it he found the path, and soon found himself at the house of a friend. The family was shocked to see him, and expressed their surprise that he had attempted such a perilous journey, since no one had ever been known to pass through that part of the wilderness in winter. Neither he nor his horse had tasted a morsel of food since they started, but they were both accustomed to hardships, and suffered only a little as a result. After obtaining some refreshment, he started to his appointment, thankful for his escape from the dangers through which he had passed [*The Life of Jacob Gruber,* pp. 39-42].

Gruber gives several incidents that occurred at camp meetings. "In one camp," he says, "some bold sinners came to fight for their master, the devil; but our captain, Immanuel, made prisoners of them, and then made them *free indeed.* One fine, strong, good-looking young man among the mourners was in great distress, and found no relief until he drew a large pistol out of his pocket, with which he intended to defend himself if anyone should offer to speak to him on the subject of religion. When he laid it on the bench beside him the Lord blessed him, and gave him a great victory over his foes" [*The Life of Jacob Gruber,* pp. 62-63].

Gruber was extremely hard on all worldliness, and especially on flamboyant fashion, which he denounced and ridiculed. A little of his healthy banter might be useful in these trendy days.

While preaching in a certain place on a certain occasion, an unusually tall lady entered. On seeing her, he stopped preaching and said, "Make room for that lady; one might have thought she was tall enough to be seen without the plumage of that bird in her bonnet." Some days later the lady met Gruber and complained that he had treated her rudely. "Oh sister," he replied, "was that you? Well, I did not know it was you; I thought you had more sense" [*The Life of Jacob Gruber,* p. 78].

At a camp meeting on a certain occasion, where considerable difficulty was experienced in getting the people to observe order – from the number of young people who were walking around, congregating in groups, and engaged in conversation – the presiding elder, in the most respectful and courteous terms, requested them to be seated. Not seeming to understand, or not caring to comply with the request, the young people paid no attention whatsoever to what was said, but continued their walking and talking. Gruber, who was present, felt greatly aggrieved, and rising in the stand he roared out, "Mr. Presiding Elder, you called those young folks gentlemen and ladies, and they obviously did not know what you meant!" He then added, "Boys, come right along and take your seats here," pointing to the right, "and you, gals, come up and take your seats here on the left." Earnest and authoritative as he was, yet so comical was his manner that their attention was instantly grabbed, and they gladly came forward and took their seats [*The Life of Jacob Gruber*, pp. 87-88].

To us this manner of speech would have seemed rude and irritating, and very unlikely to accomplish the desired end, but Jacob knew the people he had to deal with, and how to handle them. To some people a polite speech sounds like arrogance, and, taking it to mean nothing, they let it go in one ear and out the other; they yield to a plain, blunt, commanding manner of speech seen as earnestly intended. Very much depends on the character of the people to whom we speak, and also a little on our own age and position. It would never do for a young minister fresh out of college to address those of his own age as girls and boys, nor would such a style of admonition be acceptable to our educated young people even if the oldest theologian did so confront them. The practical lesson is to have the thing done somehow, if it is appropriate, and to use only such a method of speaking as will be best calculated to secure it. The dread of sinning against etiquette is as much to be avoided as the vulgarity that causes needless offense. The case in which Gruber acted so oddly will perhaps never happen to us, but, if it does, we must use our best judgment, and hope to succeed as he did.

At a camp meeting near Baltimore, after the trumpet had been blown announcing the time for closing the exercises in the praying circles, one of them, unwilling to stop, kept on singing and praying. Gruber, somewhat impatient, shouted out at the top of his voice, "That's right, brothers, blow all the fire out" [*The Life of Jacob Gruber,* pp. 88-89].

Often the same thought has come to mind when we have seen unwise brothers ranting on, long after the "spirit of supplication" (Ephesians 6:18) has been fully exhausted. Long prayers and long speeches blow out the fire they intend to increase.

Gruber's later years were more calm and quiet, but they were not quite devoid of exciting incidents. The sinners of his day were as eccentric as the preachers who sought to win them. If they were attacked from the pulpit with rough weapons, they knew how to fight for dear life in return. Gruber states,

> I was sent for a second year to the Dauphin circuit. Nothing extraordinary took place, just some guys of the lower sort made an attempt to blow up our meetinghouse in Harrisburg. On a Sunday night after preaching they got in through a window, put something with powder in it under the pulpit, and lit it with a match. It made a sound like a cannon, tore up the pulpit, and broke the glass out of some windows. We soon, however, had everything repaired, and pursued our course. My colleague that year was a poor thing hunting a fortune. He found out who was rich, but the girls found out that he was lazy, so he had little success in winning souls, and none in getting a wife. Some young men think if they can only get married (the sooner the

better), they will be at once in paradise, and some
young women have the idea that if they can only
get a preacher, they will have an angel for certain;
but more than one has been very much disappointed. [*The Life of Jacob Gruber,* p. 275]

While attending a conference in Philadelphia, in 1830, he was
asked to preach at his old charge, St. George's. He took for his
text Psalm 84:4: *Blessed are those who dwell in your house, ever
singing your praise! Selah.* Retaining a keen sense of the unkind
manner in which he was treated by some of the members there,
which resulted in his removal at the end of the first year, he felt
disposed to let his hearers know it by witty and cutting allusions. Under the topic of "The Character of those who dwell
in the House of the Lord," he mentioned three characteristics:

1. *They are a humble people,* willing to occupy a humble
   place in the church, indeed, any place so that they might
   be permitted to abide in the church; but there are some
   people who are so proud and ambitious that unless they
   can be like the first king of Israel, from the shoulders up
   higher than everybody else, they won't come into the
   house at all, but will just hang around the doors.

2. *They are a contented people.* If everything does not exactly
   suit them, they make the best of it, and try to get along as
   well as they can; but there are many who are so uneasy
   and fidgety that they can't *dwell* in the church, but are
   continually running in and out, disturbing themselves
   and everybody else.

3. *They are a satisfied people,* always finding something
   good, and thankful for it. Regardless of who their
   preacher is, they can always find something instructive
   and encouraging in the message. But some people are

never satisfied, and they are always finding fault with their preacher; some preach too loud, and some too long, and some say so many hard and strange things, and some are so drab and boring that they can't be fed at all and are never satisfied. If the multitude that were fed by the Savior had been like these people, they never would have been fed [Gruber, here, alludes to Jesus feeding the multitude (cf. Matthew 14:13-21; Mark 6:32-44; Luke 9:10-17; John 6:1-14)]. If one had cried out, "John, you won't feed me, but Peter will"; and another had said, "Andrew will feed me, but James won't"; and another, "I want all bread and no fish"; and others, "I want all fish and no bread," how could they have been fed? Such dissatisfied people cannot dwell in the house of the Lord. If they are not cast out, they will soon die out; they can't live [*The Life of Jacob Gruber*, pp. 301-302].

Though he was sometimes severe in his criticisms of young preachers, he always maintained for them a fatherly affection, and sought only to correct their errors. But we cannot think he was justified in publicly rebuking a foolish youth who had attacked Methodism, by asking the Lord "to make his heart as soft as his head, because then he might do good" [*The Life of Jacob Gruber*, pp. 353-354].

A young preacher, hoping to improve his style as a pulpit orator, and having great confidence in Jacob Gruber, wrote to him for advice. The young man had developed the habit of prolonging his words, especially when under the influence of great excitement. Deeming this the most conspicuous defect in his elocution, Gruber sent him the following terse reply:

"Dear Ah! Brother Ah! When-ah you-ah go-ah to-ah preach-ah, take-ah care-ah you-ah don't-ah say-ah Ah-ah! Yours-ah,

"Jacob-Ah-Gruber-Ah" [*The Life of Jacob Gruber*, p. 356].

But one of his oddest reproofs ever administered was on a

much larger scale, and proved very effective. In a certain church the congregation had the disgraceful practice of turning their backs to the pulpit during a certain portion of the singing. One Sunday Mr. Gruber conducted the service, and as usual the whole congregation simultaneously turned around, presenting their backs to the preacher. Instantly the preacher, to be even with them, turned around also, presenting his back to the congregation. When the time for prayer came, at the close of the hymn, the congregation was astonished to find the preacher turned away from them, gazing at the wall. The hint was enough; they did not repeat the objectionable practice again.

This is how Reverend David Martin [see Appendix A, NOTE 11B] describes the closing scene of Gruber's life:

On the evening of May twenty-third, he suddenly got worse, having several fainting attacks or collapsing. He gradually grew weaker and weaker, until forty-eight hours afterwards the scene ended. He was conscious that his death was rapidly approaching, and sighed for the happy release. He requested brother S. V. Blake [see Appendix A, NOTE 11C] – if it could be determined when he was about to die – to gather a few brothers and sisters around him, so they might (to use his own words) "See me safely off; and as I am going, all join in full chorus and sing, 'On Jordan's stormy banks I stand.'"

A few hours before he died, he asked Brother Blake whether he could hold out another night, and was answered that in his judgment he could not. "Then," he said, "tomorrow I will spend my first Sunday in heaven! Last Sunday in the church on earth, next Sunday in the church above!" and with evident emotion he added,

"Where congregations ne'er break up,
And Sabbaths have no end."[6]

Brother Blake, perceiving that he was fast sinking, and in accordance with his request, had the hymn sung that Gruber had selected; but before it was concluded he was unconscious. The singing ceased, a deathlike stillness reigned, only broken by his occasional respiration. An overwhelming sense of God's presence melted every heart. A minute more and his happy spirit winged its way to its long-sought rest. He died in the seventy-second year of his age [see Select Bibliography: cf. Wakeley, 1856, pp. 413-414].

If any judge too severely the personal peculiarities of such a man, we would urge them to do better; but to us it seems most probable that if preachers were more in earnest, we would see more of what are called eccentricities, that are often only the signs of real zeal, and the tokens that a man is both natural and intense. If a fisherman can catch fish with silk lines and artificial bait, let him be thankful; but if with a superior tackle he is unsuccessful, it shows a very proud spirit if he indulges in harsh criticisms of the style and manner of brothers who succeed better than himself in the gospel fishery. *Every man in his own order* (1 Corinthians 15:23 KJV) is a good rule. Apollos may be polished and Cephas blunt, but so long as they are honest, prayerful, and true to the gospel, God will bless them both, and it does no good for them to pick holes in each other's

---

6   Lines from the fifth stanza of the hymn, "Jerusalem, My Happy Home" (1805), written by Jeremiah Ingalls.

coats. We would never say to a man, "Be eccentric"; but if he cannot help being so, we would not have him be otherwise. The Leaning Tower of Pisa owes much of its fame to its leaning, and although it certainly is not a safe model for architects, we would by no means advise its demolition. Ten to one any builder who tried to erect another would create a huge ruin, and therefore it would not be a safe precedent; but there it is, and who wishes it was other than it is? Serve the Lord, brother, with your very best, and seek to do even better, and whatever your peculiarities, the grace of God will be glorified in you.

Chapter 12

Edward Taylor

(1793–1871)

L et us now introduce "Father Taylor," the sailor preacher of Boston. This is not Father [William] Taylor of California, who is a younger man, but Edward Taylor, pastor of Seamen's Bethel, North Square, Boston – the man whom Charles Dickens described in his *American Notes for General Circulation* [see Appendix A, NOTE 12A; also see Select Bibliography] as follows:

The only preacher I heard in Boston was Mr. Taylor, who speaks peculiarly to seamen, and who was once a mariner himself. I found his chapel down among the shipping, in one of the narrow, old, waterside streets, with a cheerful blue flag waving freely from its roof. The preacher looked a weather-beaten, hard-featured man, about fifty-six to fifty-eight years old, with deep lines chiseled as it was into his face, dark hair, and a stern, keen eye. Yet the general character of his countenance was pleasant and agreeable. His text was, *Who is that coming up from the wilderness, leaning on her beloved?* (Song of Solomon 8:5).

He handled this text in all sorts of ways, and twisted it into all different shapes, but always ingeniously, and with a rude eloquence, well adapted to the comprehension of his hearers. Indeed, if I am not mistaken, he studied their sympathies and understandings much more than what he let on. His imagery was all drawn from the sea, and from the incidents of a sea-man's life, and was often remarkably good. He spoke to them of that glorious man, Lord Horatio Nelson, and of Cuthbert Collingwood; and, as the saying goes, he drew nothing in by the head and shoulders [that is, this expression alludes to how Taylor seamlessly spoke on the seamen's level; he did not "talk over their heads," so to speak], but brought it to bear on his purpose, naturally, and with a sharp mind to its effect. Sometimes, when much excited with his subject, he had an odd way of taking his great quarto Bible [see Appendix A, NOTE 12B] under his arm and pacing up and down the pulpit with it, in the meantime looking steadily down into the midst of the congregation. As a result, when he applied his text to the first audience gathered, and pictured the wonder of the church at their presumption in forming a congregation among themselves, he stopped short with his Bible under his arm and pursued his sermon accordingly:

"Who are these – who are they – who are these fellows? Where do they come from? Where are they going to? Speak up! What's the answer?" he said, leaning out of the pulpit, and pointing downward with his right hand. "From below!" he said, starting back again; and looking at the sailors in front of him, he said, "From below, my brothers, from under the hatches of sin, battened down above you by the Evil One. That's where you come from!" He walked up and down the pulpit. "And where are you going?" he said, stopping abruptly. "Where are you going? On high!" he said very softly, and pointing upward, "On high!" he said louder. "On high!" louder still. "That's where you are going, with a fair wind, all taut and trim, steering directly for heaven in its glory, where there are no storms or foul weather, and where the wicked cease from troubling and the weary are at rest."

Another walk, and he said, "That's where you're going to, my friends. That's it. That's the place. That's the port. That's the haven. It's a blessed harbor – still water there, in all changes of the winds and tides; no driving ashore upon the rocks, or slipping your cables and running out to sea there. Peace, peace, peace, all peace!" Another walk, and putting the Bible under his left arm, he said, "What! These fellows are coming from the wilderness, are they? Yes. From the dreary, blighted wilderness of iniquity, whose only crop is death. But do they lean on anything – do they lean on nothing, these poor seamen?" Three raps on the Bible. "Ah, yes. Yes. They lean on the arm of their beloved." Three more raps. "On the arm of their beloved." Three more, and a walk. "Pilot, guiding star, and compass all in one, to all hands – here it is." Three more. "Here it is. They can do their seaman's duty manfully, and be easy in their minds in the utmost peril and danger, with this." Two more. "They can come, even these poor fellows can come, from the wilderness leaning on the arm of their beloved, and go up – up – up," raising his hand higher and higher, with every repetition of the word, until at last he stood with it stretched above his head, regarding them in a strange, ecstatic manner, and pressing the Book triumphantly to his chest, until he gradually fell back into another part of his sermon [*American Notes for General Circulation,* pp. 134-139].

We are not so enamored with Charles Dickens as to consider his verdict on a preacher to be of any real consequence with reference to the man's actual effectiveness, but as a judge of vivacity of manners, and power of style, no better critic could be found.

Mr. Taylor's first traditional (what we might call officially recognized) preaching appointment was before a quarterly

Methodist conference, assembled to test his qualifications. It has been reported that on this occasion he had the coolness to select as his text the words, *"By the life of Pharaoh, surely you are spies"* (Genesis 42:16); but his biographer says that although those words might have been worked into the sermon, the real text was a more humble but equally strange one: *"Please, let me live"* (1 Kings 20:32). He adds that the examiners saw that his passion and talents more than made up for his defects; and in answer to his prayer, they "let him live." We do not see how they could have done otherwise, since no conference would have been strong enough to kill him.

After itinerating for a number of years, the man and his mission met, and Taylor settled down in Boston, as a minister of the Methodist Episcopal Church, specifically set apart to labor among sailors. His chapel, at first, held about five hundred listeners, and was immediately filled to its maximum capacity. He began in 1828 in full revival vigor, frequently preaching four times a day. To him it never occurred to polish his style and prune away its power; he spoke as his heart prompted him, and worked as the Holy Spirit moved him. He did enough work for two men, and received a double blessing upon it. In a very short time Boston felt his power; its wealth and its culture were at his feet as well as its poverty and roughness. A noble Bethel was built for him, a house of large dimensions, a fit sphere for his operations, and by his soul-stirring ministry he made "the Bethel" famous in all lands.

It was not at all amazing that sailors especially, and other classes of the community in tow, would flock to hear Mr. Taylor, since he was a man of great human sympathies, masculine, bold, honest, childlike, and outspoken, and, at the same time, a man on fire with love for Christ and lost souls. His preaching could never be dull – the intense white heat of his nature prevented that. He was extraordinarily earnest, and commanded the attention of all around him for that very reason.

No ideas of propriety, or notions of delicacy, hung around him like chains. He spoke to sailors, not to squeamish aristocrats; and to "the sons of Zebulon" (Genesis 49:13) he poured out his great heart in a plain eloquence that was completely on fire. A man who heard him in 1835 reported,

> His eloquence was marvelous; his control over the audience seemed almost absolute. Tears and smiles chased each other over our faces like the rain and sunshine of an April day. He had one of the most brilliant imaginations that ever sparkled and burned. His sermon was all poetry, though it came in bursts and jets of flame. It was like the dance of the aurora, changing all the while from silver flame to purple, and back again. But the secret of his magnetic power lay in his overflowing sympathies that leaped over all barriers, and had no regard for time or place. There was no wall of formality between him and his hearers, any more than if he were talking to each one of us in a private room. He would single out a person in his audience, and talk to him individually with the same freedom as if he met him in the street. "Ah! my jolly tar" [see Appendix A, NOTE 12C], turning to a sailor who just then happened to catch his eye, "here you are, in port again; God bless you! Watch your helm, and you will reach a fairer port by and by. Listen! Don't you hear the bells of heaven over the sea?"

We think, rightly so, that ridiculousness was allowed considerable play in his sermons. To the pure mind, none of the powers of our fortitude are common or unclean. Humor can, and should, be consecrated. We grant that it is a power difficult to manage, but when it is under proper control, it more than repays for all the labor spent on it. Children do sad damage with gunpowder, but what a force it is when a wise man directs its energy. Mr. Taylor made men laugh so that they might weep. He touched one natural chord so that he might be able to touch another, whereas some preachers are so unnatural themselves, that the human nature of their listeners refuses to subject itself to their operations. Oh you who are forever prudishly dull, before you judge a man whose loving ministry guided thousands to the skies, consider how he soared immeasurably higher than you all, and remember that with all his violations of your miserable regulations, he was one whom the Lord delighted to honor. Farthing candles laugh at the sun for its spots, unaware that those spots are excessive light; and they may be quite sure of another thing – that spots or no spots, ten thousand glimmers such as theirs are not worthy to be compared with the stray beams of the great orb of day [see Appendix A, NOTE 12D].

At the prayer meetings, Taylor – like a father among his own family – cast off all restraint, and unveiled his inner nature with childlike bluntness. One of his most amazing displays of this kind was after a speech by a visitor who related the death of an incredibly evil man who was blown up a few days before in a powder mill at Wilmington. He came down crushed and mangled, and gave his heart to God; and now who would not say with the holy man of old, *"Let me die the death of the upright, and let my end be like his!"* (Numbers 23:10)? Taylor suddenly stood up. "I don't want any trash brought into this altar. I hope none of my people decide on serving the devil all their lives and cheating him with their dying breath. Don't look forward to honoring God by giving Him the last snuff of an expiring candle. Perhaps you will never be blown up in a powder-mill." He continued: "That holy man whom we heard speak was Balaam, the meanest scoundrel mentioned in the Old Testament or the New. And now I hope we shall never hear anything more from Balaam, nor from his donkey."

His own prayers – full of imagery – were more like the reflections of a Far Easterner, than a son of these colder Western climates. Consider his prayer at the dedication of a new church: "If any man attempts to sow heresy in this pulpit, or to preach anything but Christ and Him crucified, Lord, drive him out of the house and sweep his tracks off the floor." The Sunday before he was to sail for Europe, he was asking the Lord to take good care of his church during his absence. All of a sudden, he stopped and exclaimed, "What have I done? Distrust the Providence of heaven? A God that gives a whale a ton of herrings for breakfast, will He not care for my children?" And then he went on, closing his prayer in a more confiding strain.

His work in one particular field is not generally known. Living at the North End of Boston, near the lowest haunts of vice, he was often called to attend the deathbeds of abandoned women. Protected by his eccentricity and his purity equally from any shadow of suspicion, he always obeyed such summons. At all hours of the day or night he visited the gloomiest haunts of crime in this noble service, never with one harsh word for the fallen, never with any apology for their crime. He received many warnings against going on such errands. The only concession he ever made was to lay aside his cane; everywhere else it was his constant companion, but he never took his cane with him when he visited the cellars and garrets of North Street. This was simple courage in the Christian soldier, but it was also the wisest prudence [cf. Gilbert Haven and Thomas Russell, *Father Taylor, the Sailor Preacher*, 1872, pp. 313-314].

It grieves my heart to relate that after many years of glorious service, Taylor faded away little by little over the course of ten long years – slowly, but surely, losing all his powers. It was as the Lord would have it; but to drift around as a poor hulk, with the armament removed, and the light in the binnacle extinguished, was very traumatic to both the old man and to his friends.

So passed away the one whom Ralph Waldo Emerson called one of the two greatest poets of the United States. He was a pedobaptist [one who advocates infant baptism], an Arminian, and a man of a thousand divergences from our line of things that we believe to be more scriptural than his; yet, despite all that, we cast a funeral wreath with no grudging hand on the coffin of a good and true man, and say, "Would to God there were others to fill his place!"

Chapter 13

Edward Brooke

(1799–1871)

Our Wesleyan brothers have recently lost from their ministry an eminently useful preacher, who was the last survivor of a little band of simplehearted and downright sincere men, who in their day were mighty soul winners, but had the reputation of being somewhat eccentric. William Dawson and Samuel Hick were worthily perpetuated in Squire Edward Brooke, who entered into rest in January 1871. Do not suppose that we endorse all his theology, nor do we applaud all his modes of procedure; we have no patience with those who imagine that you cannot admire a man's character unless you agree with him in every doctrinal sentiment. Mr. Brooke was soundly abused in his day, and certain libelous papers attributed the most outrageous conduct to him; but, in truth, he was just a plain and somewhat quaint preacher of the old, old gospel, and his Master clothed him with great power.

Squire Brooke came from a wealthy Yorkshire family that owned a considerable estate among the wild moorlands of

Northern England. His parents belonged to the established church while Edward was in his boyhood, but were brought to know the Lord in later years by the preaching of their zealous son. Edward was not sent to Eton College or Harrow School, as he should have been; instead, following the bent of his inclination, he was allowed to remain on the farm to fish and hunt and shoot, and to develop a fine constitution and a mind all his own. Amid the rocks and the heather, the forest trees and the ferns, Edward Brooke, with his dogs and his gun, found both sport and health; or dashing over the country after the hounds, he enjoyed sheer exhilaration and trained his courage in the hunt. Up to the age of twenty-two he seems to have been completely devoid of any religious thought; but as we Calvinists are inclined to put it, the time appointed by the Lord drew near, and sovereign grace issued its warrant of arrest against him, resolving in infinite love to make him a captive to its power.

[The following excerpts in this chapter come exclusively from Reverend John Holt Lord's *Squire Brooke. A Memorial of Edward Brooke, of Fieldhouse, near Huddersfield, with Extracts from His Diary and Correspondence,* 1873; see Select Bibliography.]

Early in the year 1821, Edward Brooke woke up one morning, intent on pleasure. Equipped for his favorite sport, with gun in hand and followed by his dogs, he was crossing the Honley Moors, when a lone man met him with a message from God. The man was a Primitive Methodist preacher named Thomas Holladay, one of those strong-minded, earnest evangelists, the validity of whose orders is disdainfully denied by many, but who, judged by the results of their ministry, hold a commission higher than bishops can bestow – a commission signed and sealed by He who is *head over all things to the church* (Ephesians 1:22).

Intent on his Master's work, *in season and out of season* (2 Timothy 4:2), Holladay was ready to seize an opportunity of usefulness. Passing the young sportsman, he respectfully greeted him and said with the sincerest of pity, "Sir, you are seeking happiness where you will never find it." The man of God went on, perhaps little imagining that the arrow – though a shot in the dark – had pierced the joints of the armor encasing the young sportsman's heart. Yet it was so.

The wounded sportsman went home, the words of Holladay still sounding in his ears: "Sir, you are seeking happiness where you will never find it." The time was right. It was a day of visitation for that neighborhood. The Spirit of God was moving on the population. A great revival was in progress [*Squire Brooke. A Memorial of Edward Brooke,* pp. 10-11].

The awakened young gentleman began to attend cottage prayer meetings and to speak with the godly men of the neighborhood, and as a result, his anxiety was greatly deepened, and his desire for salvation inflamed.

It was the day of his sister's wedding. Ill-prepared to join in the festivities of the occasion, because of the sorrow of his heart, Edward Brooke spent hours the previous night in reading his Bible and wrestling with God for salvation.

> All night the lonely suppliant prayed,
> All night his earnest crying made.[7]

Around four o'clock in the morning, while kneeling by the old armchair in his father's kitchen, still pleading for mercy through the mediation of Jesus, his soul grew desperate, and like Jacob wrestling with the angel until the break of day, he resolved, "*I will not let you go unless you bless me*" (Genesis 32:26).

That strong persistence was the manifestation of true faith. He was enabled to receive Jesus as his Savior, and believing with his heart, he was justified. These words were applied to his heart as distinctly and seriously as if spoken by a voice from heaven:

---

7   Opening lines to the poem, "The Suppliant," by Richard Chenevix Trench

"Your many sins are all forgiven; go, and from now on, sin no more" (cf. John 8:11). Every fear and sorrow vanished, and, believing, he rejoiced with joy unspeakable and full of glory.

Elated over his amazing deliverance, his first impulse was to make it known. He hurried to his sister's room and told her the happy news that Christ had saved him – a glorious announcement on her wedding day. Then, even though it was early, he ran out into the village and woke a praying man named Ben Naylot, whose heart he knew would be in sympathy with his, and told him how he had found the Lord. The two of them then called up a third, named Joseph Donkersley, to share their joy. From the rejoicing trio there arose a song of praise; the jubilant and sweet notes were as music in God's ear, and prompted the songs of angels, and gave new incentive to the happiness of heaven, since *there is joy before the angels of God over one sinner who repents* (Luke 15:10) [*Squire Brook. A Memorial of Edward Brooke*, pp. 14-15].

From that moment Edward Brooke was what he would have called "a bran' new man." He could do nothing halfway; once and for all, he renounced everything that had been a part of his former way of life. Finding field sports to have too great a charm for him, he abandoned them in the most resolute manner. He remarked to a Christian friend, "I found that the gate was narrow (cf. Matthew 7:14), and so I pressed into it myself, and left my horses, my dogs, and the world outside." In his zeal to be through with what he felt to be a temptation, he gave orders to have his dog kennels pulled down. On hearing this, his father intervened and countermanded the instructions, saying, "I hope Edward will want the kennels again." But it was in vain; the die was cast, the camel had gone through the needle's eye (cf. Luke 18:25) and could not come back through such a narrow passage. Edward Brooke frequently attended cottage prayer meetings, talked with the workers at the mill, exhorted others in his father's kitchen, and instructed travelers by the roadside. He began, in fact, to put himself in training to become *a mighty hunter before the* Lord (Genesis 10:9), and a consecrated Nimrod whose game would be the souls of men.

Mr. Brooke's early career illustrates the great effectiveness of small meetings in rooms and cottages, where the uneducated, the poor, and the newly converted could feel at home in their first attempts at speaking. Had it not been for these gatherings, he might have remained silent, since he never would have dared to deliver his first sermons in front of a large congregation. Our author [John Holt Lord] wisely remarks, "The cottage prayer meeting is certainly one of the best training schools for the development of Christian gifts. In some of our town circuits, where chapels are few and large, and the pulpits invariably supplied by ordained ministers, and where Sunday-afternoon services have been discontinued, and no rooms or cottages are opened for mission work, what opportunity have those whom the Spirit moves to preach His Word, to test their call by actual experiment, and to develop their preaching power by frequent practice?" [*Squire Brooke. A Memorial of Edward Brooke,* p. 41].

In such meetings, Edward Brooke first endeavored to share the message of salvation, that was like a fire burning in his bones, until he was no longer able to contain himself; and there he found encouragement and strength for further ministry [*Squire Brooke. A Memorial of Edward Brooke,* p. 42].

After prayerful consideration and consultation with Christian friends, arrangements were made for Edward Brooke to submit his convictions of duty to the judgment of others, by preaching in James Donkersley's chamber, a large room that answered the threefold purpose of a workshop, a bedroom, and a place where the neighbors might gather to worship God. The service was duly announced, and great interest was piqued in the young squire's first appearance as a preacher. The chamber was crowded, and many hearts were lifted up in earnest prayer that God would encourage and help His young servant in this first trial of his pulpit gifts. The preacher selected for his text a passage in harmony with his intense convictions: *The wicked shall be turned into hell, and all the nations that forget God* (Psalm 9:17 KJV). Acting on a sense of duty, and humbly relying on God, the preacher was divinely assisted, and the effort was a success [*Squire Brooke. A Memorial of Edward Brooke*, pp. 54-55].

The sensational news that the young squire had started to preach soon spread throughout the neighborhood and district. Opportunity to exercise his gifts was offered on every hand, which he accepted as a call from God. Those who had known the squire in his wild days, and those who had simply heard of his remarkable conversion, all flocked to hear him. The announcement that Squire Brooke would preach not only drew young squires, but also emptied the pubs far and near. It was the signal for many old poachers, dogfighters, pigeon flyers [see Appendix A, NOTE 13A], drunkards, and habitual Sabbath breakers to find their way to the house of God. The squire attracted congregations unlike anything that others could get, comprising the wild men, the publicans and harlots, and the roughs and rejects of society, the sight of whom, in the house of God, must have made the heart of the preacher leap for joy, and carried him out of himself.

Influenced by the strange character of the congregations that crowded around to hear him, and by the fact that many heard him, to whose uneducated and carnal minds theological terms and doctrinal definitions conveyed no meaning, and ordinary preaching was unintelligible, he, of set purpose, renounced the style of his first sermon in favor of another, which but for the preacher's motive and exceptional position, might be open to criticism, and which, in a scribe, would be most reprehensible [*Squire Brooke. A Memorial of Edward Brooke*, pp. 55-56].

We cannot pretend to give even an outline of Mr. Brooke's long and useful life, but must satisfy ourselves with citing incidents that illustrate both his eccentricity and his enthusiasm. He gradually abandoned all his worldly pursuits for the sake of soul winning, and having an ample fortune he traveled far and wide, paying his own way, and preaching the gospel *without money and without price* (Isaiah 55:1) – a mode of life that we both admire and envy. In his journeys, and at other times, he was always on the lookout for individual cases, which he dealt with in his own manner, and with remarkable success. Note the following anecdotes:

One of the members of the Sheepridge Mutual Improvement Society [see Appendix A, NOTE 13B] unfortunately messed with hard liquor, until his enemy got the best of him. He was found one day in a pub, indulging in free drinks; and since his wife's persuasions failed to bring him out, she went to the squire to ask for his intervention.

Immediately, the squire followed the grieving woman to the pub, and walked right in, where a number of old drunks were soaking according to their custom; and there, in the middle of them, was the fallen man. "What are you doing here?" said the squire, fixing his eyes on the poor backslider. "This is no place for you." Disturbed by Mr. Brooke's unexpected appearance, and conscience stricken, the man gave no reply, and seemed as though he would have gladly dropped through a hole in the floor to escape the terrifying gaze of the squire's reproving eyes. "Step outside with me; it's time you go home," said the squire, and as the culprit remained seated, he seized him by his coat collar and dragged him out into the street.

The drunks, infuriated by such an encroachment on the man's "personal liberties," jumped to their feet and rushed to the rescue. The squire turned around, looked his opponents in the face, and raising his big, powerful arm, said, "There is not a man in the bunch who dares lay a finger on me." He then walked off with his prisoner, gave him good counsel, and there is reason to believe that he never fell into the snare of alcohol again [*Squire Brooke. A Memorial of Edward Brooke*, p. 169].

Driving to an appointment on a beautiful Sunday morning in spring with Mr. D. Smith, a Sheffield local preacher and a colleague in labor, Mr. Brooke suddenly said, "Pull up, Smith." Mr. Brooke then stood up in the carriage and shouted to a man in a distant part of a field by the roadside, who was gathering nettles. "Here, I want you," he said, simultaneously beckoning with his hand for the man to come to him. When he came up to the fence, Mr. Brooke said, "You poor foolish sinner, are you going to sell your precious soul to the devil on a Sunday morning for a few paltry nettles?" And looking earnestly into his face, he prayed with great solemnity, "The Lord have mercy on your soul. Amen." Then, quick as a wink, he said, "Drive on, Smith." When well on the way again, he said, "I could not let that man sell his soul for nettles without warning him" [*Squire Brooke. A Memorial of Edward Brooke*, p. 175].

Driving to some village in Derbyshire, where he was expected to preach in the afternoon, the squire pulled up at a roadside inn. Having seen that his horse was fed, he ordered his usual meal of ham and eggs. A fine, healthy-looking young country-man entered the room and sat down to rest. The squire made some friendly observations, and when his meal was served, he invited the young man to join him. The offer was gratefully accepted. While enjoying their wholesome meal together, the youth's heart opened, and there was a pleasant flow of conversation. "We are expecting a very strange preacher," he said, "at our village tonight. He is a great man for prayer meetings, and tries to convert all the folks into Methodists."

"Indeed," replied the squire, with evident interest in the topic, "have you ever listened to him?"

"No, I haven't," said the youth, "but my brother has."

"Well, what did your brother say about him?" inquired the squire.

"Oh, he told me he never heard such an odd chap in his life; indeed, he didn't know if he was quite right in his head, but," said the young man, "I intend to go and hear for myself."

"That is right, my boy," said the squire, "and get your brother to go too, for he may have a word to suit you both." They did go, and greatly to the young man's surprise, as the preacher mounted the pulpit, he recognized his friendly host at the wayside inn. As the squire proceeded with the service, the young man's heart was touched, as was his brother's. At the prayer meeting they were found among the repentant seekers of salvation, and were both converted not only into Methodists, but also into Christian believers [*Squire Brooke. A Memorial of Edward Brooke,* pp. 178-179].

Here is an example of his distinctive letters – brief, but all on fire:

> Dear John, In reply to yours, I ask permission to say that our labor at Honley was not in vain. A new class has been formed, and about a dozen have joined it. Two found peace. Praise the Lord! We shall rise. All hell is on the move, but we must go around the bulwarks of our Zion, and mark her palaces well, and we will ultimately and finally triumph over all. I say *all.* Continue, John, in the work. Live near to God. Be a giant in religion, one of the first and best men in your day. Plead with God. Live in the glory. "Advance" is the Christian's motto. Onward to certain victory over sin, the world, and hell. Trample down worldly, fashionable conformity. Know the will of God and do it. Do it heartily, cheerfully, fully, eternally, and heaven will be your guide, defense, and all in all. Our kind respects.

And in your prayers, remember

Edward Brooke.[8]

We regrettably say farewell to Squire Brooke, as we copy the last entry from his diary:

> *"In returning and rest you shall be saved; in quietness and in trust shall be your strength"* (Isaiah 30:15). *"You will see greater things than these"* (John 1:50). *"You meet him with rich blessings"* (Psalm 21:3). *"I will . . . do more good to you than ever before"* (Ezekiel 36:11). *My soul is even as a weaned child* (Psalm 131:2 KJV)

And then, possibly to express his fuller grasp of the infinite mercy of his covenant God, and a firmer trust than he had previously experienced, he writes with a trembling hand that was soon to forget its dexterity, "Never before" [*Squire Brooke. A Memorial of Edward Brooke*, p. 267].

There is no wonder that his memoir is in its fourth edition; it is exceedingly well written, and we congratulate Mr. Lord on his spirit and ability.

---

8   Squire Brooke. A Memorial of Edward Brooke, p. 229.

Chapter 14

Billy Bray, the Uneducated
Soul Winner

(1794–1868)

Many Christians who are prepared to tolerate, and even to admire, considerable diversities of character, have yet, unconsciously to themselves, laid down in their own minds very rigid and precise limits within which those diversities will range. So far, they are still looking for a measure of uniformity, and will probably require several more or less violent jolts of their propriety before they will be able to admit within the circle of their sympathy various eccentric and erratic forms of authentic spiritual life that, nevertheless, have had their uses, and have brought no small glory to God. Most of us are somewhat tolerant of well-educated eccentrics; we almost revere the oddities of genius, but we are squeamish if we see peculiarities combined with ignorance, and idiosyncrasies prominent in men who cannot even spell the word. What in a gentleman would be a peculiarity, is reckoned in a poor man to be an absurdity. Most men are such slaves to kid gloves and accurate scales at the banker's, that they kowtow to aristocratic whims, and effectively admire in my *Lord Havethecash* that which would disgust them in poor *Tom Honesty*. This partiality of judgment, in short, affects even Christians, who, beyond all other people, are bound to judge things by their own intrinsic value, and not according to the false glitter of position and wealth. We claim for uneducated Christians as wide a range for their originality as would be allowed them if they were the well-instructed children of the rich; we would not have a shrewd saying maligned because it is ungrammatical, nor a heartfelt, spiritual utterance ridiculed because it is roughly expressed. Consider the man as he is; make allowances for educational disadvantages, for circumstances, and for companionships, and do not turn away with contempt from that which, in the sight of God, may be infinitely more precious than all the refinements and delicacies so dear to pompous imbecility.

With this long-winded preface we now introduce a few notes on William Trewartha Bray, of Cornwall, for several years a local preacher among the Bible Christians [see Appendix A, NOTE 14A]. We beg his pardon for calling him by a name that he never used, and introduce him a second time, with due accuracy, as Billy Bray. This honorable man was once a drunken and lascivious miner, but grace made him an intensely earnest and unwavering follower of the Lord Jesus. His conversion was very remarkable, and was accompanied with those violent struggles of conscience that frequently accompany that great change in strong-minded and passionate personalities.

His actual obtaining of peace brought tears to our eyes as we read it, and made us remember a boy who, more than twenty years ago, found the Lord in a somewhat similar fashion. It also reminded us of George Fox the Quaker, and John Bunyan the Baptist, when undergoing the sacred change. Children of God are born very much alike; their divergences usually arise as a matter of ensuing years. In their regeneration, as in their prayers, they appear as one. Bray was assaulted by the fierce temptation that he would never find mercy; but with the promise, *Seek, and you will find* (Matthew 7:7), he extinguished this flaming dart of the Evil One (cf. Ephesians 6:16), and in due time he learned, by blessed experience, that the promise was true. His own words are beautifully simple and touching.

> I said to the Lord, "You have said, *'Ask, and it will be given to you; seek, and you will find; knock, and it will be opened to you'* (Matthew 7:7), and I have faith to believe it." In an instant the Lord made me so happy that I cannot express what I felt. I shouted for joy. I praised God with my whole heart for what He had done for a poor sinner like me, since I could say, the Lord has pardoned all my sins. I think this was in November 1823, but what day of the month I do not know. I remember this, that everything looked new to me – the people, the fields, the cattle, the trees. I was like a man in a new world. I spent the majority of my time praising the Lord. I could say with David, *[The Lord] drew me up from the pit of destruction, out of the miry bog, and set my feet upon a rock, making my steps secure. He put a new song in my mouth, a song of praise to our God* (Psalm 40:2-3). I was a new man altogether. I told everyone I met what the Lord had done for my soul. I have heard some say that they have to work hard to get away from their companions, but I had to work hard to find them soon enough to tell them what the Lord had done for me. Some said I was crazy, and others that they would get me back again next payday. But, praise the Lord, it is now over forty years later,

and they have not got me yet. They said I was a *mad*
man, but they meant I was a *glad* man, and, glory be
to God! I have been glad ever since. [F. W. Bourne,
The King's Son; or, A Memoir of Billy Bray, 1887, p. 9]

No sooner was Billy saved than he instantly began looking after
others. He prayed for his workmates, and saw several brought to
Jesus in answer to his prayer. His was a simple faith; he believed
in the reality of prayer. He meant his prayers to be heard, and
expected them to be answered whenever he pleaded for the
souls of his comrades. He was a man alive, not a mannequin.
In his own simple style he did all that he did with rigor, physical robustness being more than sufficiently conspicuous in his
shouting and leaping for joy. He tells us, soon after his conversion, "I was very happy in my work, and could leap and dance
for joy underground as well as on the surface" [see Appendix
A, NOTE 14B].

About a year after Bray's conversion, he began publicly to
exhort men to repent and turn to God. Towards the end of 1824,
his name was put on the Local Preachers' Plan, and his labors
were greatly blessed in the conversion of souls. He typically did
not select a text, as is the normal habit of preachers; instead,
he typically began his addresses by reciting a verse of a hymn,
sharing a little of his own experience, or telling an anecdote.
But he had the happy art of pleasing and profiting all classes,
the rich as much as the poor; and all characters, the worldly
as much as the devout, flocked to hear him. He retained his
popularity until the end [*The King's Son; or, A Memoir of Billy
Bray*, p. 18].

Perhaps no preacher in Cornwall ever acquired more extensive or more lasting renown; and the announcement of his name
as a speaker at a missionary meeting, or on any special occasion, was a sufficient attraction, whoever else might or might

not be present. Sometimes his illustrations and appeals made a powerful impression.

I remember once hearing him speak with great effect to a large congregation, primarily miners. In that neighborhood there were two mines, one very prosperous, and the other quite the opposite, since the work was hard and the wages low. In his sermon he represented himself as working at *that* mine all the week, but on payday going to the prosperous one for his wages. "Had he not been at work at the other mine?" the manager inquired. He had, but he liked the wages at the good mine the best. He pleaded very earnestly, but in vain, and was dismissed with the remark – from which there was no appeal – that he must come there to work if he wanted to come there for his wages. And then Bray turned towards the congregation, and the effect was almost irresistible, saying that they must serve Christ here if they would share His glory hereafter, but if they would serve the devil now, they must go to him for their wages by and by. It was certainly a very simple illustration, but one that convinced the understanding and subdued the hearts of his listeners [*The King's Son; or, A Memoir of Billy Bray,* p. 19].

There was excitement in some of his meetings, more than sufficient to shock the prejudices of highly sensitive or refined people. Some, even those who had the fullest confidence and warmest affection for Billy, could not enjoy some of the outward manifestations they occasionally witnessed to the extent that he himself did. Billy could not tolerate *deadness,* as he expressively called it, either in a professing Christian or in a meeting. He had deeper sympathy with people singing or shouting or leaping for joy than he had with

> The speechless awe that dares not move,
> And all the silent heaven of love.[9]

---

9   Charles Wesley, "Sinners, Obey the Gospel Word" (c. 1749), tenth stanza
    The King's Son; or, A Memoir of Billy Bray, p. 21

Methodism is the mother church of Cornwall, and Bray was a genuine though uncultivated child of her heart. As John Wesley always associated the grace of God with the penny-a-week, so Bray's religion was not all shouting; it had an eminently practical turn in many directions.

Billy was quite a mighty chapel builder; he began by getting a piece of freehold [see Appendix A, NOTE 14C] from his mother, that he cleared with his own hands, and then proceeded to dig out the foundations of a chapel that was to be called Bethel (cf. Genesis 35:7). Under great discouragements, both from friends and foes – mostly, however, from the former – he actually built the place, working at it himself, and at the same time begging for stone, begging for timber, and begging for money to pay the workers. He gave all the little he had, and prompted all around him, who had anything to spare, to give likewise. Onlookers thought Billy was silly, and called him so; but, as he well remarked, "Wise men could not have preached in the chapel if silly Billy had not built it." Almost as soon as one building was finished, he was motivated to start another. It was much needed, and many talked about it, but nobody had the heart to initiate it except Billy Bray. He begged for the land, borrowed a horse and cart from a benefactor, and then after doing his own hard day's work underground in the pit, and providing for five small children, he and his son worked at raising stone and building the walls, frequently working twenty hours of the twenty-four. He endured a hard struggle over this second chapel, but his own account is best:

"When our chapel was about up to the doorhead, the devil said to me, 'They are all gone and have left you and the chapel. If I were you, I would go and leave the place too.' Then I said, 'Devil, I thought you knew me better than that; by the help of the Lord I will have the chapel up, or die trying.' [In Spurgeon's original text, Billy Bray concludes his response to the devil with this obscure idiom: 'or loose my skin on the down.'] So the devil spoke no more to me on that subject. Sometimes I had blisters on my hands, and they have been very sore. But I felt I did not mind that, since if the chapel should stand one hundred years, and if one soul was converted in it every year, *that* would be a hundred souls, and that would pay me well if I got to heaven, since they that *turn many to righteousness [shall shine] like the stars forever and ever* (Daniel 12:3). So I thought I should be rich enough when I got there.

"The chapel was finished after a time, and the opening day came. We did have preaching, but the preacher was a wise man, and a dead man. I believe there was not much good done that day, since it was a very dead time with the preacher and people, since he had a great deal of *grammar,* and only a little of *Father.* 'Not by might, nor by power, but by my Spirit, says the LORD of hosts' (Zechariah 4:6). If it was by wisdom or might, I should have but a small part, since my might is little and my wisdom less. Thanks be to God, the work is His, and He can work by whomever He pleases.

"The second Sunday after the chapel was opened, I was 'planned' there. I said to the people, 'You know I did not work here building this chapel in order to fill my pocket, but for the good of the neighbors, and the good of souls; and souls I must have, and souls I will have.' The Lord blessed us in a wonderful manner. Two women cried to the Lord for mercy, and when I saw that, I said, 'Now the chapel is already paid for.' The good Lord went on to work there, and the society soon went up from fifteen members to thirty. You see how good the Lord is to me; I spoke for one soul a year, and He gave me fifteen souls the first year. Bless and praise His holy name, for He is good, and His mercy endures forever, since one soul is worth a thousand worlds.

"Our little chapel had three windows, one on one side, and

two on the other. The old devil, who does not like chapels, put it on his servants, by way of reproach, to call our chapel *Three-Eyes*. But, blessed be God, since then, the chapel has become too small for the place, and it has been enlarged. Now there are six windows instead of three, and they may call the chapel *Six-Eyes* if they will. Since then, glory be to God, many who have been converted there are now in heaven; and, when we get there, we will praise Him with all our might, and he shall never hear the last of it."

No sooner was this second house finished than he began a third and larger one, and in this enterprise his talent for collecting, as well as his zeal in giving and working, were well displayed. He had high – and as we believe proper – ideas of his mission, in organizing the pledged contributions of the Lord's stewards.

A friend who was with Billy on a begging expedition suggested, as they were coming near a gentleman's house, and Billy was evidently heading for the front door, that it would be better if they went to the back door. "No," said Billy, "I am the son of a King, and I shall go frontways" [*The King's Son; or, A Memoir of Billy Bray*, p. 52].

One time, at a missionary meeting, Billy seemed quite annoyed because there was something said in the report about money received for "rags and bones." When he rose to address the meeting, he said, "I don't think it is right supporting the Lord's cause with old rags and bones. The Lord deserves the best, and should have the best" [*The King's Son; or, A Memoir of Billy Bray*, pp. 104-105].

Well done, Billy! This is good, sound divinity.

Billy knew how to fight the devil and his agents with their own weapons. Returning late from a revival meeting, on a dark night on a lonely road, "certain lewd fellows of the lower sort" tried to scare him by making all sorts of unearthly sounds, but he went singing on his way. At last one of them said, in the most terrifying tones, "But I'm the devil up here in the hedge, Billy Bray." "Bless the Lord! Bless the Lord!" said Billy. "I did not know you were so far away as that." To use Billy's own expression, "What could the devil do with someone like [him]?" [*The King's Son; or, A Memoir of Billy Bray*, p. 86].

One of the most blessed results of his deep piety was his genuine humility and his continual sense of dependence on God. The Lord's servants without the Lord's presence are weak like other men, like Samson, when he lost his locks. Here is one experience of Billy's:

"When I was in the St. Neots Circuit, I was on the plan, and I remember that one Sunday I was planned at Redgate, and there was a chapel full of people, and the Lord gave me great power and liberty in speaking. But all of a sudden the Lord took His Spirit away from me, so that I could not speak a word, and this might have been the best sermon that some of them ever heard. 'What!' you say, 'and with you looking like a fool and unable to speak?' Yes, since it was not long before I said, 'I am glad I was stopped, and that for three reasons. The first is: to humble my soul, and make me feel more dependent on my Lord; to think more fully of the Lord and less of myself. The next reason is: to convince those of you who are ungodly, since you say we can speak what we have a mind to, without the Lord as well as with Him. But you cannot say so now, since you hear how I was speaking, but when the Lord took His Spirit away, I could not say another word; without my Lord I could do nothing. And the third reason is: that some of you young men who are standing here may be called to stand in the pulpit someday as I am, and the Lord may take His Spirit from you just as He did from me, and then you might say, 'It is no good for me to try to preach or exhort, since I was stopped the last time I tried to preach, and I shall preach no more.' But now you can say, 'I saw poor old Billy Bray stopped once like me, and he did not mind it, and he told the people that he was glad his Lord had stopped him. Billy Bray's Lord is my Lord, and I am glad He stopped me too, since if I can benefit the people and glorify God, that is what I want.' I then spoke a great while, and told the people what the Lord gave me to say" [*The King's Son; or, A Memoir of Billy Bray,* pp. 110-111].

Preaching in such a spirit Bray was sure to have a blessing, and a blessing he had. Many orators and doctors in divinity look very small by the side of Billy Bray, if we estimate ministries by their results in soul winning; and they will look smaller still when the souls saved by poor humble speakers shall shine forth like stars, and their own oratorical fame and boasted learning shall be as darkness.

We say no more, but refer the reader to the memoir of Billy Bray, written by Mr. F. W. Bourne, and published at the Bible Christian Book Room, 57, Fairbank Street, East Road.

In Conclusion

All these eccentric preachers were outrightly earnest, and because they were so, their humor sometimes stood out. Had their consecration to their work been less complete, they would have taken more thought of public opinion, and would have been more fearful of incurring reproach. But they were so set on their one object of sending home the truth to the consciences of their listeners that they forgot their own reputations, and spoke with boldness.

Had these men been triflers with holy things, or jokers on sacred topics, they would have been worthy of all the criticism that has been thrown at them; but they were nothing of the kind. Among the earnest they were the most earnest; no one can doubt that. This, indeed, lay at the bottom of the opposition that they aroused. Had they been only jokers, the world would not have hated them as much as it did, since it loves those who make it all fun and games. Had they cultivated a prim feebleness, or had they been content to perform their office with the lifelessness of routine, they would have run no risk of standing in the stocks of scorn, since men may be as dull and as powerless as they please in the ministry without fear of being called eccentric.

If all men were right-minded, they would be willing to listen to the message of salvation, even if it was couched in the driest terms of technical theology; but men are so careless about all the matters of their souls that we have to not only preach to them, but also induce them to hear us. A great part of our labor lies in seeking out attractive illustrations, parables, and select sayings, by which we may coax men to attend to their own interests; and even then we fail, unless a higher power intervenes. We would be content to preach moralistic truth with unwavering solemnity if the multitude would just hear us, but they will not. What then? If the healing medicine is nauseous to the child, we must sweeten the potion or brighten the pill. If our words will not run by themselves, we must put them on wheels to set them in motion. Our object is – if by any means we may save some; and since men will not believe without hearing, and will not hear unless we make the Word pleasant and attractive to them, we dare not do otherwise than indulge them in this respect, and woo them to instruction as children are enticed to learning by stories and pictures.

This little book is not written to promote eccentricity, or even to excuse all its displays, but rather, if possible, to take the edge from the scalping knife of slanderous misrepresentation and griping criticism. Fair and constructive criticism is not to be denigrated; it may be useful if honestly and kindly spoken. No Christian minister in his right mind wishes to shield himself behind his office, nor does he desire to be regarded as infallible; but what we do request is that our listeners' thoughts not be diverted from our subject by the little details of our style and demeanor. These are trifles, but our message is a matter of life and death.

Reader, if you are brought to believe in the Lord Jesus Christ, you will find very little fault with the ministry that has led to so desirable a consummation; and if you are a hearer of the gospel and still reject the Savior, you will not be able to make an excuse for your unbelief out of the peculiarity of the preacher, since in these days if one man cannot profit you, it is easy for you to find another, and there is no law to prevent your going where you are most benefited. Better shift your seat than waste your Sundays.

To all wise and candid believers we offer the language of the apostle: *What then is Apollos? What is Paul? Servants through whom you believed, as the Lord assigned to each* (1 Corinthians 3:5). They are not to be pitted against one another, as if they were rivals engaged in fighting for the belt; they are to be loved, helped, and prayed for as coworkers of our faith. *So let no one boast in men. For all things are yours, whether Paul or Apollos or Cephas or the world or life or death or the present or the future—all are yours, and you are Christ's, and Christ is God's* (1 Corinthians 3:21-23)

[The original concludes: "Passmore & Alabaster, Printers, 81, Little Britain, E.C."]

Acknowledgements

This book would not have been possible without the help and work of a great many people. In particular, I would like to thank my wife, Fawne Metheny, for her continuing love and support of her *eccentric preacher* husband in all that he sets his mind to do, as well as my son, Dylan Thomas Metheny, who encouraged his old man to go the distance in citing this book's original sources as exhaustively as possible. To Chad Baggett, Jared Baker, and John Galyen, thank you for your friendship, the incessant – yet always somehow supportive – group texts, and those Thursday-morning breakfast distractions from the centric world; *Iron,* indeed, *sharpens iron, and one man sharpens another* (Proverbs 27:17). And Chad, thank you for taking on the role as beta reader for this revision – to further express my appreciation, I'll use your catchphrase: "That's awesome!" Thanks also to Kyle Reeder for contributing the foreword to this edition – terrific job, my friend – and to the staff at Aneko Press for going the extra mile to get this little project of mine published.

Select Bibliography

"A Concise Account of the Life of the Rev. Daniel Burgess" (1833). In *The Miscellaneous Works of the Rev. Matthew Henry, V.D.M. Volume 2.* Joseph Ogle Robinson (Internet Archive). <https://archive.org/details/miscellaneouswo02henrgoog/page/n8/mode/2up?view=theater>

Alexander, et al. (1863). *The Imperial Dictionary of Universal Biography: A Series of Original Memoirs of Distinguished Men, of All Ages and All Nations, Volume 3.* William Mackenzie (Google Books). <https://books.google.com/books?id=hzMOAAAAQAAJ&printsec>

Arundel, et al. (1829). *The Evangelical Magazine and Missionary Chronicle 1829. Vol. VII.*—New Series. (Google Books). <https://play.google.com/books/reader?id=fFsoAAAAYAAJ&pg=GBS.PP2>

Bogue, D. and Bennett, J. (1809). *History of Dissenters, from the Revolution in 1688, to the Year 1808, Volume 2.* B. Tilling. (Google Books). <https://books.google.com/books?id=P1kQAAAAIAAJ&printsec>

Bourne, F. (1874). *The King's Son; or, A Memoir of Billy Bray. Third Edition.* Hamilton, Adams, & Co. (Internet Archive). <https://archive.org/details/MN40270ucmf_0/page/n9/mode/2up>

Chalmers, A. (1813). *The General Biographical Dictionary: Containing an Historical and Critical Account of the Lives and Writings of the Most Eminent Persons in Every Nation, Particularly the British and Irish, from the Earliest Accounts to the Present Time, Volume 7.* J. Nichols & Son. (Google Books). <https://books.google.com/books?id=Dp9jAAAAMAAJ&pg=PA318&lpg=PA318&dq>

Charlesworth, V. (1876). *Rowland Hill; His Life, Anecdotes, and Pulpit Sayings.* Hodder and Stoughton. (Internet Archive). <https://

archive.org/details/rowlandhillhisl00socigoog/page/n12/
mode/1up>

Cunningham, A. (1866). *The Poetical Works of Robert Burns with Life,
Notes, and Glossary.* Davis, Porter, and Coates (Internet Archive).
<https://ia800200.us.archive.org/20/items/poeticalworksofr-
01burnsro/poeticalworksofr01burnsro.pdf>

Dickens, C. (1842). *American Notes for General Circulation, Volume 1.*
Chapman and Hall. (Google Books). <https://books.google.com/
books?id=owolAAAAMAAJ&printsec>

Grant, J. (1839). *The Metropolitan Pulpit: Or, Sketches of the
Most Popular Preachers in London, Volume 1.* George
Virtue (Google Books). <https://play.google.com/books/
reader?id=lHkEAAAAQAAJ&pg=GBS.PR1&hl=en>

Haven, G. and Russell, T. (1872). *Father Taylor, the Sailor Preacher:
Incidents and Anecdotes of Rev. Edward T. Taylor, for Over Forty
Years Pastor of the Seaman's Bethel, Boston.* B. B. Russel (Internet
Archive). <https://archive.org/details/in.ernet.dli.2015.88734/
mode/2up>

Hymns by John Berridge (Updated: February 21, 2021). Precept Austin.
<https://www.preceptaustin.org/hymns_by_john_berridge>

Jones, W. (1845). *Memoir of the Rev. Rowland Hill, M.A. Third Edition.*
Henry G. Bohn. (Google Books). <https://books.google.com/
books?id=56AEAAAAYAAJ&printsec>

Larwood, J. (1871). *The Book of Clerical Anecdotes or, the Antiquities,
Humours, and Eccentricities of "the Cloth."* John Camden
Hotten (Google Books). <https://books.google.com/
books?id=bBrFb18DRbkC&printsec>

Latimer, H. *The Third Sermon of M. Hugh Latimer, Preached before King
Edward, March twenty-second, 1549.* Christian Classics Ethereal
Library.
<https://ccel.org/ccel/latimer/sermons/sermons.vii.iii.html>

Lingard, J. (1840). *A History of England from the First Invasion
by the Romans to the Accession of William and Mary in
1688. Fifth Edition, Volume Three.* Baudry's European
Library. (Google Books). <https://books.google.com/

books?id=9ow9AAAAYAAJ&pg=RA2-PA354&lpg=RA2-PA354&dq>

Lord, J. (1873). *Squire Brooke. A Memorial of Edward Brooke, of Fieldhouse, near Huddersfield, with Extracts from His Diary and Correspondence.* Hamilton, Adams, & Co. (Google Books). <https://books.google.com/books?id=16E5AQAAMAAJ&printsec>

Middleton, E. (1807). *Evangelical Biography: Being a Complete and Faithful Account of the Lives, Sufferings, Experiences & Happy Deaths of Eminent Christians, who Have Shone with Distinguished Lustre; Alphabetically Arranged with Lists of Their Principal Works, in Chronological Order and Occasional Extracts, Volume 1.* J. Stratford. (Google Books). <https://play.google.com/books/reader?id=_WADAAAAYAAJ&pg=GBS.PR6&hl=en>

Peters, H. (1683). *A Dying Father's Last Legacy to An Only Child, Or, Mr. Hugh Peters' Advice to His Daughter.* William Marshall (Internet Archive). <https://archive.org/details/bim_early-english-books-1641-1700_a-dying-fathers-last-leg_peters-hugh_1683/mode/2up>

Sermons by the Late Mr. William Dawson, of Barnbow near Leeds (1860). William Walker and Sons (Google Books). <https://books.google.com/books?id=dV5oAAAAcAAJ&printsec=frontcover&source=gbs_ge_summary_r&cad=0#v=onepage&q&f=false>

Spurgeon, C. (1978). *Eccentric Preachers.* Pilgrim Publications. (Internet Archive). <https://archive.org/details/eccentricpreache00spur/mode/2up>

Strickland, W. (1860). *The Life of Jacob Gruber.* Carlton and Porter. (Google Books). <https://www.google.com/books/edition/The_Life_of_Jacob_Gruber/paazX1IT1eEC?hl=en&gbpv=1>

Taylor, W. (1859). *The Model Preacher.* Swormstedt and Poe. (Google Books). <https://books.google.com.pa/books?id=nmEyAQAAMAAJ&printsec=frontcover#v=onepage&q&f=false>

Timbs, J. (1890). *English Eccentrics and Eccentricities.* Chatto and Windus. (Internet Archive). <https://archive.org/details/englisheccentric00timbiala/page/n5/mode/2up>

"The Fifth Sermon upon the Lord's Prayer, Made by Master Hugh Latimer (Matthew 6:9)" (1824). In *The Sermons of the Right Reverend Father in God, and Constant Martyr of Jesus, Hugh Latimer, Volume 2.* James Duncan (Google Books). <https://play.google.com/books/reader?id=-DsFIs4oBLYC&pg=GBS.PA1&hl=en>

"The Fourth Sermon of Master Latimer's (Philippians 3:17-18)" (1844). In Rev. G. E. Corrie's (Ed.) *Sermons by Hugh Latimer.* Cambridge University Press (Google Books). <https://books.google.com/books?id=6YNsTHCd-hMC&pg=PA524&lpg=PA524&dq=#v=onepage&q&f=false>

The Tales and Jests of Mr. Hugh Peters (1660/1807). Printed for S. D./ Reprinted for J. Caulfield (Google Books). <https://books.google.com/books?id=TLU_AAAAcAAJ&printsec>

The Whole Works of the Rev. John Berridge, A.M. Second Edition, with Additions (1864). Ebenezer Palmer (Google Books). <https://books.google.com/books?id=JBZXAAAAcAAJ&printsec>

Wakeley, J. (1856). *The Heroes of Methodism: Containing Sketches of Eminent Methodist Ministers, and Characteristic Anecdotes of their Personal History.* Carlton and Porter. (Google Books). <https://books.google.com/books?id=jNI-AAAAYAAJ&printsec>

Wells, C. (1905). *A Satire Anthology.* Charles Scribner's Sons. (Wikipedia.org). <https://upload.wikimedia.org/wikipedia/commons/a/a3/A_satire_anthology_%28IA_satireanthology00well%29.pdf>

Whittingham, R. (1838). *The Works of the Rev. John Berridge: With an Enlarged Memoir of His Life; Numerous Letters, Anecdotes, Outlines of Sermons, and Observations on Passages of Scripture; And His Original Sion's Songs.* Simpkin, Marshall and Company. (Internet Archive). <https://archive.org/details/worksofrevjohnbe00berrrich/page/n7/mode/2up>

APPENDIX A

Additional Notes

Spurgeon's Preface

NOTE 0A: "My book on Commenting and Commentaries"
Commenting and Commentaries (1876) was the second of "The College Series" of published works "useful to Students and Ministers" prepared and fully endorsed by Charles Spurgeon himself. The first volume was Spurgeon's *Lectures to my Students: a Selection from Addresses delivered to the Students of the Pastors' College, Metropolitan Tabernacle* (1875).

Johnson, P. (2001). *Commenting & Commentaries by Charles H. Spurgeon.* The Spurgeon Archive. <http://www.romans45.org/spurgeon/misc/c&c.htm>

Chapter 1: "What Is Eccentricity?"

NOTE 1A: "Chips in the porridge"
This (now obscure) nineteenth-century English expression appears to denote an addition that is so insignificant or unimportant as to have virtually no effect. As to the etymology of the idiom, some argue that *porridge* was originally *pottage*, that is, a thick vegetable soup or stew, and that *chip* is used in its older

sense of a paring of breadcrust, that would add substance but little flavor to the soup.

Smith, J. B. (February 1996). "'Bees Up Flues' and 'Chips In Porridge': Two Proverbial Sayings in Thomas Hardy's 'The Return of the Native,'" *The Thomas Hardy Journal,* 12 (1), 52-56.

NOTE 1B: "Lady Day, Midsummer Day,
Michaelmas Day, and Christmas Day"

England's business year was first divided into four "Quarter Days" during the Tudor period. These dates on the English calendar – March 25th (Lady Day), June 24th (Midsummer Day), September 29th (Michelmas Day), and December 25th (Christmas Day) – were close to solstices or equinoxes and divided the year into four equal quarters. All debts and lawsuits had to be settled and a public record made by the quarter day.

Guthrie, N. (June 2019). *What Are Quarter Days & Why Do We Use Them?* Timms Solicitors. <https://www.timms-law.com/commercial-property-what-are-quarter-days/>

Lady Day: A Quarter Day and The New Year: March 25 (April 20, 2021). Agecroft Hall & Gardens. <https://www.agecrofthall.org/single-post/lady-day-a-quarter-day-and-the-new-year-march-25>

NOTE 1C: "Half a grain"

One of the earliest units of common measure and the smallest, a "grain" is a uniform unit in the avoirdupois, apothecaries', and troy systems. It is a unit of measurement of mass equal to approximately 0.065 grams, or 1/7,000-pound avoirdupois; therefore, "half a grain" is equivalent to approximately 0.0325 grams, or 1/14,000-pound avoirdupois.

Grain, Unit of Weight. Britannica (Britannica.com). <https://www.britannica.com/science/grain-unit-of-weight>

NOTE 1D: "Droneingen"

This obscure term is perhaps a play on, or a misspelling of, the

Norwegian word *dronningen* (translated "the Queen"). Hence, Spurgeon's statement, "You will earn yourself a high degree in the great university of Droneingen," is (presumably) an expression of his disdain towards the droning degree-holders from Queens' College, University of Cambridge, England.

Results for Dronningen Translation from Norwegian to English (2023). My Memory by Translated Labs. <https://mymemory. translated.net/en/Norwegian/English/dronningen>

That Apostrophe (2023). Queens' College Cambridge. <https://www.queens.cam.ac.uk/visiting-the-college/history/ college-facts/that-apostrophe>

Chapter 2: "Who Has Been Called Eccentric?"

NOTE 2A: *"Little Bethel"*

That is, a Nonconformist chapel, especially a Baptist or Methodist one; a small church boasting great spiritual influence among its surrounding community, but of minor historical importance overall (nationally). The phrase, in such senses, is uniquely British and it appears to have been most prominently used during the Victorian era in which Spurgeon lived. Charles Dickens also used the expression in his serial novel, *The Old Curiosity Shop* (1840–1841).

Corfield, W. (October 1, 1913). "Where Was Little Bethel?" *The Dickensian*, 9 (10), 268. ProQuest. <https://www.proquest.com/openview/81281967d06cd4d1574cd795b10a6475/1 ?pq-origsite=gscholar&cbl=1818261>

NOTE 2B: *"Ranters"*

Ranters were members of a loosely organized mid-seventeenth-century group of quasi-Christian anarchists, whose antinomian tendencies – such as their unbridled dancing, drinking, smoking, swearing, and sharing of sexual partners – scandalized most other dissenting English sects (for example, the Puritans).

They were known to widely produce and distribute prophetic tracts, among other writings, a few of which still exist today. However, through lack of organization and the extreme hostility of magistrates and ministers, their heyday was short-lived. The term *Ranters* was also later used colloquially to describe the Primitive Methodists.

Cannon, J., Crowcroft, R. (Eds.). (2015). *A Dictionary of British History* (3rd ed.). Oxford University Press.

Bowker, J. (2000). *The Concise Oxford Dictionary of World Religions.* Oxford University Press.

NOTE 2C: "Tenterden steeple was the cause of the Goodwin Sands"

This unique phrase is a once-popular satirical retort when some ridiculous reason is given for a thing. The expression comes from an old English legend that connects the church of St. Mildred's tall, massive, perpendicular tower (located at Tenterden) with Goodwin Sands, a ten-mile-long sandbank located along the English Channel that has long been notorious for the danger it poses to ships of all kinds. The legend is that the abbot of St. Augustine, Canterbury, diverted the funds by which the seawall protecting Earl Godwin's island was maintained, for the purpose of building Tenterden steeple, the consequence being that in 1099, a great flood occurred and "Tenterden steeple was the cause of the Goodwin Sands."

Shipwrecks. Goodwin Sands Conservation Trust. <https://goodwinsands.org.uk/why-so-important/history-heritage/shipwrecks/>

Tenterden—Encyclopedia. Theodora.com. <https://theodora.com/encyclopedia/t/tenterden.html>

NOTE 2D: "The Gray Friars"

The Gray Friars, or Franciscans, were followers of Saint Francis of Assisi (d. 1226). They earned their name from the gray habits that were worn as a symbol of their vow of poverty.

History of the Greyfriars in Great Britain and Ireland. The Greyfriars: The Order of Friars Minor Conventual of Great Britain and Ireland. (thegreyfriars.org). <https://www.thegrey-friars.org/history>

NOTE 2E: "Strike"

That is, an obsolete unit of volume once used for dry measure in the United Kingdom. Since the term originated, it has at times been associated with varying amounts of measurement by volume; per Hugh Latimer's usage, it indicated about two bushels' worth.

Manuscripts and Special Collections: Volumes or Capacities. University of Nottingham (UK). <https://www.nottingham. ac.uk/manuscriptsandspecialcollections/researchguidance/ weightsandmeasures/volumes.aspx>

Chapter 3: "Causes Of Eccentricity"

NOTE 3A: "Dr. William Bengo Collyer's chapel"

In January 1802, at the age of nineteen, William Bengo Collyer (1782–1854) began preaching in a large but almost empty building at Peckham, London. Under his ministry the church began to grow rapidly in the next six years. Dr. Collyer's congregation reached over one thousand, and royalty regularly worshiped in what became known as "Hanover Chapel."

Dr. William Bengo Collyer. Find a Grave. <https://www. findagrave.com/memorial/16916715/william-bengo-collyer>

NOTE 3B: "Metropolitan Tabernacle"

The [new] Metropolitan Tabernacle, located at Elephant and Castle (London, England), was the site where Spurgeon's congregation gathered for worship at the time of his writing *Eccentric Preachers* (1879). The building, which was completed in 1861, featured an auditorium seating six thousand people. Records indicate that by the time of Spurgeon's death, the membership at his church was over fifty-three hundred.

About Elephant and Castle: Spurgeon and the Metropolitan Tabernacle (no date – A version of this article was first published in the *Elephant* magazine, Spring 2022). Elephant and Castle Partnership. <https://www.elephantandcastle.org.uk/a-brief-history/metropolitan-tabernacle/>

Chang, G. (June 14, 2023). *How Spurgeon Got His Congregation.* TGC (The Gospel Coalition). <https://www.thegospelcoalition.org/article/spurgeon-got-congregation/>

Chapter 4: "Hugh Latimer"

NOTE 4A: *"The Black Friars"*

The Black Friars (or Dominicans) were so-called because they wore long, black mantles over their white robes. As a sect, they were particularly engaged with preaching and charitable work with the laity; their monastery in London was a venue for early parliamentary conclaves. Henry VIII dissolved the Order in England in 1538.

Blackfriars, City of London. (2023). Hidden London. <https://hidden-london.com/gazetteer/blackfriars/>

NOTE 4B: *"Bluff Hal"*

That is, a popular nickname for King Henry VIII, since *Harry* is often a nickname for *Henry* (among the British), and *Hal* is derived from *Harry,* and *bluff* as an adjective means "cheerful." Henry was notably happy, athletic, and easygoing for the first part of his life. But by the time of his death in 1547, the once-fit King Henry was neither looking nor feeling his best.

"Bluff" Hal had become "Bloated" Hal as a result of a jousting accident in 1536, which left him with an ulcerated leg that prevented him from exercising.

Day, M. (March 19, 2010). *Bluff King Hal.* St. Margarets. <https://stmargarets.london/archives/2010/03/bluff_king_hal.html>

Chapter 5: "Hugh Peters"

NOTE 5A: "The Restoration"
That is, the Restoration of England's monarchy in 1660, marked by the return of Charles II as king, following the period of Oliver Cromwell's republican Commonwealth (c. 1649–1660).

The Restoration. Royal Museums Greenwich. <https://www.rmg.co.uk/stories/topics/restoration>

NOTE 5B: "The so-called Great Rebellion"
The "Great Rebellion" is another name for the English Civil War, which was a catastrophic series of conflicts that took place in the middle of the seventeenth century. Fought between those loyal to King Charles I and those loyal to parliament, the conflicts divided the nation at all levels of society. At the heart of the war were fundamental questions concerning power and religion. "The so-called Great Rebellion," as Spurgeon deems it, was, and remains today, one of the most controversial episodes in the history of England.

The English Civil Wars: History and Stories. English Heritage. <https://www.english-heritage.org.uk/learn/histories/the-english-civil-wars-history-and-stories/>

NOTE 5C: "St. Sepulchre's Church"
St. Sepulchre's Church is located near the Old Bailey in London. It is also called St. Sepulchre-without-Newgate because it formerly stood just outside of the city wall near Newgate Prison. St.

Sepulchre's has been a popular church since its first construction in the twelfth century. Most notably, one of St. Sepulchre's vicars played an important role in history: Reverend John Rogers was the first martyr during Queen Mary's reign; he was burned at the stake for his religious beliefs.

Simons, K. (2017). *St. Sepulchre without Newgate Church*. Fordham University. <https://medievallondon. ace.fordham.edu/exhibits/show/medieval-london-sites/ stsepulchrewithoutnewgatechurc>

NOTE 5D: *"The fall of Basing House"*

Basing House, Hampshire, was an opulent private residence that became a royalist stronghold during the English Civil Wars. Its "fall" on October 14, 1645, was a major parliamentarian victory.

Siege of Basing House. British Battles (British battles. com). <https://www.britishbattles.com/english-civil-war/ siege-of-basing-house/>

Chapter 6: "Daniel Burgess"

NOTE 6A: *"Sacheverell's mobs"*

A reference to the Sachaverell Riots that erupted in London's West End on the night of March 1, 1710, following the third day of the impeachment of Dr. Henry Sacheverell (1674–1724). This outspoken high Anglican and Oxford professor was on trial at Westminster Hall for preaching and publishing a sermon condemning the Whig government for its favoritism towards Dissenters. Rioters demonstrated their sympathy for the doctor by looting and burning six prominent dissenting meetinghouses. According to Spurgeon's source(s), Daniel Burgess's chapel was one among the six meetinghouses "completely wrecked" that night.

Alison, M. (May 12, 2021). *Henry Sacheverell's Progress*.

Shropshire Archives. <https://www.shropshirearchives.org.uk/blog/henry-sacheverells-progress/>

Cannon, J. (2009). *Oxford Dictionary of British History* (3rd ed). Oxford University Press.

NOTE 6B: "The Society for the Reformation of Manners"
The Society for the Reformation of Manners was formed in 1690. Led by prominent politicians and religious leaders – with the support of the Protestant royals William and Mary – the Society sought to prevent vice by using the courts aggressively to punish those who committed a range of offenses, including profane swearing and cursing, sabbath breaking, drunkenness, "lewd and disorderly" conduct, brothel keeping, gaming, and sodomy. Since ordinary people and even officers such as constables could not be counted on to prosecute such offenders, the reformers encouraged informers, some of whom were paid a salary, to take up the mantle. Ultimately, though, widespread opposition to the use of informers to enforce the Gin Act (1736) dealt the Society a death blow; it disappeared from the historical record in 1738.

Reformation of Manners Campaigns (2018). London Lives 1690 to 1800 (londonlives.org). <https://www.londonlives.org/static/Reformation.jsp>

NOTE 6C: "Morning exercises"
These were informal, Nonconformist worship gatherings held around London (most prevalently) during the reign of Charles II (reigned 1660–1685). Such meetings were relatively small, usually held at 7:00 a.m., and almost always in public places. They lasted for an hour, with the time split between prayer and preaching. History seems to suggest that the "famous series of 'morning exercises'" said to have featured Daniel Burgess's preaching, were those held at Cripplegate – one of the most notable gates in London. This series of meetings had a consistent leadership,

but would also feature guest appearances from well-known men. John Milton, John Foxe, Oliver Cromwell, John Bunyan, Richard Baxter, William Cooper, Stephen Charnock, John Owen, Thomas Manton, Thomas Vincent, Thomas Watson, and Matthew Poole all at some point led the morning exercises at Cripplegate.

Why Cripplegate? (2023). The Cripplegate. <https://thecripplegate.com/why-cripplegate/>

Chapter 7: "John Berridge"

NOTE 7A: "Prunella"

According to *Brewer's Dictionary of Phrase and Fable* (oxfordreference.com), *Prunella* is defined as "a dark, smooth, woolen stuff of which clergymen's and barristers' gowns used to be made."

Dent, S. (Ed.) (2013). *Brewer's Dictionary of Phrase and Fable* (19th ed.): *Prunella*. Chambers Harrap Publishers. (Oxford Reference). <https://www.oxfordreference.com/display/10.1093/acref/9780199990009.001.0001/acref-9780199990009-e-8578;jsessionid=3814965530323E77224BA6ED53918EB4>

Chapter 8: "Rowland Hill"

NOTE 8A: "Lord George Gordon's Protestant rowdies"

That is, a reference to the "Gordon Riots." On June 2, 1780, a crowd of forty thousand to fifty thousand people associated with the Protestant Association gathered in St. George's Fields, London, with their leader, Lord George Gordon, to march to parliament with a petition to repeal the Catholic Relief Act. This bill, passed in 1778, lifted restrictions on the civil rights of Roman Catholics to expedite their recruitment into the military, so that the British Army had more personnel to suppress the American colonies. This reasoning, however, was dismissed by the majority of the British populace, who were mostly Protestant. Mass disapproval of parliament's actions, in turn, erupted into the most destructive urban outbreak in British history.

History of the Gordon Riots. Georgia Southern University (College of Arts and Humanities / Digital Humanities). <https://georgiasouthern.libguides.com/c.php?g=602478&p=5463809#>

NOTE 8B: "Vernon J. Charlesworth . . .
has written a life of Rowland Hill"
The actual title of Charlesworth's book is *Rowland Hill; His Life, Anecdotes, and Pulpit Sayings* (1876). Spurgeon, who "promised and vowed to write no prefaces for anybody," made an exception in the case of his friend Charlesworth's volume on Rowland Hill. The book's original cover proudly boasted, "WITH AN INTRODUCTION BY C. H. SPURGEON."

Charlesworth, V. (1876). *Rowland Hill; His Life, Anecdotes, and Pulpit Sayings.* Hodder and Stoughton. (Internet Archive). <https://archive.org/details/rowlandhillhisl00socigoog/page/n12/mode/1up>

NOTE 8C: "The Saturday"
That is, *The Saturday Magazine,* a British (Anglican) periodical that ran for 801 issues from July 7, 1832 to December 28, 1844. The magazine was encyclopedic in nature, and was purportedly published as a way for the working man to educate himself; but its content came not without its share of denominational bias.

The Saturday Magazine. HathiTrust. <https://catalog.hathitrust.org/Record/000675300>

Chapter 9: "Matthew Wilks"

NOTE 9A: "Both tabs"

That is, both tabernacles; a reference to the two Whitefieldite Chapels in London during Wilks's lifetime, where he was known to preach: the Moorfield Tabernacle and Tottenham Court Chapel. A wonderful little letter, handwritten by Matthew Wilks and dated 1826, was posted (online) for sale in 2023. In the letter, Wilks writes to William Orme informing him that he has accidentally invited him to preach at Tottenham Court Chapel when he meant to invite him to the Moorfield Tabernacle on the eighteenth of February. So, he is scheduling him at "both tabs," and praises the preaching of his friend.

1826 MATTHEW WILKS. 1.5p ALS to William Orme from George Whitefield's Successor! (2023). Specs Fine Books. <https://specsfinebooks.com/products/1826-matthew-wilks-1-5p-als-to-william-orme-from-george-whitefields-successor>

Whitefield's Tabernacle. A Dictionary of Methodism in Britain and Ireland. <https://dmbi.online/index.php?do=app.entry&id=2676>

NOTE 9B: "Williams the martyr at Erromango"

Erromango is the fourth-largest island in the Vanuatu (New Hebrides) archipelago. John Williams was the first British missionary to land there, but immediately upon his landing he was attacked by the island's inhabitants who were cannibals.

Graves, D. (May 3, 2010). *John Williams Martyred on Erromanga.* Christianity.com. <https://www.christianity.com/church/church-history/timeline/1801-1900/john-williams-martyred-on-erromanga-11630456.html#google_vignette>

Chapter 10: "William Dawson"

N/A (No additional notes).

Chapter 11: "Jacob Gruber"

NOTE 11A: "The German Reformed Church"
Historically, Martin Luther's "Ninety-five Theses," published in 1517, laid the foundations for Protestantism and the subsequent development of the German Reformed Church. From the beginning of the eighteenth century, the German Reformed Church played a vital role in developing the religious landscape of southeastern Pennsylvania (Jacob Gruber's place of origin). The church's aim in America was to provide a spiritual home for early German immigrants and their children that, over time, also served as a medium for adapting to American culture, even as many congregations supported their own schools and social services, and retained German as a language in worship and basic education through the nineteenth century.

Gaydosh, B. (2020). *German Reformed Church*. The Encyclopedia of Greater Philadelphia. <https://philadelphiaencyclopedia.org/essays/german-reformed-church/>

NOTE 11B: "Reverend David Martin"
It is interesting to note that in addition to Martin's anecdote that Spurgeon includes in his closing remarks to his chapter on Gruber, David Martin, pastor of the Fredericktown (Maryland) Methodist Church, also famously published a record of the *Trial of Rev. Jacob Gruber, Minister in the Methodist Episcopal Church, at the March Term, 1819, in the Frederick County Court, for a Misdemeanor* (1819). Gruber's trial took place on account of his having been arrested in 1818 for preaching a camp-meeting sermon that was a strong indictment of slavery; the official charge was inciting slaves "to resist the lawful authority of their . . . respective masters and lawful owners." The text that Strickland (and consequently, Spurgeon) cites as Martin's description of "the closing scene of Gruber's life" also appears in Joseph Beaumont Wakeley's book, *The Heroes of Methodism: Containing*

Sketches of Eminent Methodist Ministers, and Characteristic Anecdotes of their Personal History (1856); however, Wakeley fails to acknowledge Martin as the anecdote's source.

Martin, D. (1819). *Trial of Rev. Jacob Gruber, Minister in the Methodist Episcopal Church, at the March Term, 1819, in the Frederick County Court, for a Misdemeanor.* George Kolb. (Library of Congress). <https://www.loc.gov/resource/rbcmisc.lst0094/?st=gallery>

Wakeley, J. (1856). *The Heroes of Methodism: Containing Sketches of Eminent Methodist Ministers, and Characteristic Anecdotes of their Personal History.* Carlton and Porter. (Google Books). <https://books.google.com/books?id=jNI-AAAAYAAJ&printsec=frontcover&source=gbs_ge_summary_r&cad=0#v=onepage&q=Martin&f=false>

NOTE 11C: "Brother S. V. Blake"

No biographical details existing at this time. Spurgeon in his original text mentions this "brother" only by his surname; both Strickland and Wakeley add to that knowledge his first and middle initials. *A History of the Methodist Episcopal Church, Volume IV,* by Dr. Nathan Bangs, lists a "Samuel V. Blake" as one "received 1830" among preachers "into full connection in the Methodist Episcopal Church" from the years 1762 to 1840. Presumably, this is the same "brother S. V. Blake" who attended to Gruber on his deathbed.

Bangs, N. (1840). *A History of the Methodist Episcopal Church: An Alphabetical List of the M. E. Preachers 1762–1840.* Christian Classics Ethereal Library. <https://ccel.org/ccel/bangs/alphabetic/alphabetic.i.i.html#i.i-p10.201>

Wakeley, J. (1856). *The Heroes of Methodism: Containing Sketches of Eminent Methodist Ministers, and Characteristic Anecdotes of their Personal History.* Carlton and Porter. (Google Books). <https://books.google.com/books?id=jNI-AAAAYAAJ&printsec>

Chapter 12: "Edward Taylor"

NOTE 12A: "American Notes for General Circulation"
Charles Dickens' *American Notes for General Circulation* is a travelogue detailing his trip to the New World from January to June 1842. While there, he acted as a critical observer of North American society, almost as if returning a status report on its progress. Friends and enemies on both sides of the Atlantic considered the publication his greatest failure.

Dickens, C. (1842). *American Notes for General Circulation, Vol. 1, Second Edition.* Chapman and Hall. (Internet Archive). <https://archive.org/details/americannotesfo07dickgoog/page/n7/mode/2up>

NOTE 12B: "Great quarto Bible"
That is, a Bible bound in quarto, a book size about 9½ x 12 in. (24 x 30 cm), determined by folding printed sheets twice to form four leaves or eight pages.

Quarto. Dictionary.com. <https://www.dictionary.com/browse/quartos>

NOTE 12C: "Tar"
That is, a sailor. The word, in this instance, is a shortened variant of the seafaring word *tarpaulin,* which originated as a compound of the words *tar* and *palling,* referring to a tarred canvas pall used to cover objects on ships. Sailors often tarred their own overcoats, hats, and trousers in the same manner as the sheets or palls. By association, sailors became known as jack tars, or simply, tars.

Jack Tar: Myth and Reality (2011). *More Than a List of Crew* (Maritime History Archive). <https://mha.mun.ca/mha/mlc/articles/introducing-merchant-seafaring/jack-tar.php>

Jack Tars and Tarpaulin (July 28, 2015). Royal Museums Greenwich. <https://www.rmg.co.uk/stories/blog/library-archive/jack-tars-tarpaulins>

NOTE 12D: *"Farthing candles"*

The term *farthing* is an old English word meaning "a fourth thing." As a form of British currency, a farthing was once the smallest and least valuable coin in circulation (except for a twenty-seven-year period in the mid nineteenth century under Queen Victoria, when there was a half-farthing), worth only a quarter of the British penny. Thus, Spurgeon's expression, "farthing candles," most likely denotes the smallest and least expensive type of candles that a consumer might buy in nineteenth-century England.

Manuscripts and Special Collections: Money. University of Nottingham. <https://www.nottingham.ac.uk/manuscript-sandspecialcollections/researchguidance/weightsandmeasures/money>

Reuben, A. (May 31, 2019). *What is the Least Valuable British Coin Ever?* BBC (bbc.com). <https://www.bbc.com/news/business-48153442>

Chapter 13: "Edward Brooke"

NOTE 13A: *"Pigeon flyers"*

Pigeon flyers were those individuals who took part in – and most likely wagered on – the sport of racing specially trained homing pigeons from a predetermined distance. The sport of pigeon flying (aka "pigeon racing") was obviously a very popular pastime in Northern England during the nineteenth century,

Getting Started (2023). Royal Pigeon Racing Association. <https://www.rpra.org/about-rpra/getting-started/>

NOTE 13B: *"Sheepridge Mutual Improvement Society"*

Mutual improvement societies began in London at the end of the Napoleonic Wars and spread to the north of England around 1825. Such societies were democratic and usually provided instruction by working men themselves in elementary sub-jects. Political discussion was also a major feature, and many of the more liberal societies turned to socialism by the 1890s. Their decline began around 1900, and like so many Victorian institutions, they largely passed away with the coming of the First World War.

Pattern, D. (Last modified: May 2019). *Mutual Improvement Societies.* Huddlesfield Exposed. <https://huddersfield.exposed/wiki/Mutual_Improvement_Societies>

Radcliffe, C. (1997). "Mutual Improvement Societies and the Forging of Working-class Political Consciousness in Nineteenth-century England." *International Journal of Lifelong Education,* 16 (2), 141-155.

Chapter 14: "Billy Bray, the Uneducated Soul Winner"

NOTE 14A: "Bible Christians"

Bible Christians, also known as Bryanites, was an association of English Wesleyan Methodists founded in 1815 in North Devon by William O'Bryan, a local Cornish preacher who had extended his evangelism beyond the limits of his own circuit. Bible Christians were so named for their habit of carrying Bibles under their arms, which they persistently used in both private devotion and public worship. The movement spread rapidly during the nineteenth century and was widely engaged in foreign missionary work.

Birth and Rebirth of Joyful Billy Bray (April 28, 2010). Christianity.com. <https://www.christianity.com/church/church-history/timeline/1701-1800/birth-and-rebirth-of-joyful-billy-bray-11630326.html>

Livingstone, E. A. (Ed.) (2006). *The Concise Oxford Dictionary of the Christian Church* (2nd ed.). Oxford University Press.

NOTE 14B: "I . . . could leap and dance for joy underground as well as on the surface"

Billy Bray's enthusiastic statement alludes to his longtime vocation as a miner; even in his mining work, his elevated spirit was intense. He often claimed, "As I go along the street, I lift one foot and it seems to say, 'Glory!' and I lift the other, and it seems to say, 'Amen!' And they keep on like that all the time I'm walking." Until the age of seventy-three, he'd share with practically everyone this blessed quote: "Jesus has made me glad and no one can make me sad. Jesus makes me shout and no one can make me doubt. Jesus makes me dance and leap and there's no one that can keep down my feet."

Malkin, B. (November 13, 2021). *Billy Bray's Incredible Testimony.* Preacherbrotherbob.com. <http://preachbrotherbob.blogspot.com/2021/11/billy-brays-incredible-testimony.html>

NOTE 14C: "A piece of freehold"

That is, a plot of land. Merriam-Webster defines *freehold* (British) as an estate held in fee simple; *fee simple* being a legal term used in real estate that means full and irrevocable ownership of land, and any buildings on that land.

Freehold, (2). Merriam-Webster Dictionary (merriam-webster.com). <https://www.merriam-webster.com/dictionary/freehold>

Taylor, M. (November 28, 2023). *What Is Fee Simple Ownership In Real Estate?* Bankrate (bankrate.com). <https://www.bankrate.com/real-estate/what-is-fee-simple/>

In Conclusion

N/A (No additional notes).

Glossary of "Eccentric Preachers" and Other Notables

A

Adams, Zabdiel (1739–1801): Zabdiel Adams was a Congregational minister of Lunenburg, Massachusetts, and a cousin to the second U.S. President, John Adams (1735–1826; president 1797–1801).

Alexander, William Lindsay (1808–1884): William Lindsay Alexander was a Scottish Congregational minister, theologian, lecturer, author, and hymnist.

Asbury, Francis (1745–1816): Francis Asbury was one of the first two bishops of the Methodist Episcopal Church in the United States. He is believed to have preached over sixteen thousand sermons and traveled over a quarter of a million miles as a circuit-riding evangelist.

Askew, "Lady" Anne (1521–1546): "Lady" Anne Askew was an English (Protestant) writer, poet, and feminist. She was a pawn in a plot to implicate suspected Protestant-leaning women at the court of King Henry VIII, including the queen herself, Katherine Parr. Anne, aged twenty-five, was burned at the stake at Smithfield on July 16, 1546.

B

Bates, William (1625–1699): William Bates was an English Presbyterian minister, held to be the "politest" of all Nonconformists.

Berridge, John (1716–1793): John Berridge was an Anglican evangelical revivalist and hymnist, well regarded as "the peddler of the gospel."

Binney, Thomas (1798–1874): Thomas Binney was an English Congregational minister who actively sought reunion with the Church of England. He brought his chapel services closer to those of the established church by introducing the chanting of psalms taken from the King James Version of the Bible.

Blair, John (d. 1782): John Blair was an Anglican minister and chronologist best known for his numerous printings, reprintings, and editions of *The Chronology and History of the World*.

Blomfield, Charles James (1786–1857): Charles James Blomfield was a British theologian, classicist, and Anglican bishop. As bishop of London, Blomfield made strenuous efforts to improve the provision of churches, clergymen, and schools in England's capital; he aroused controversy by his attempts to compromise with the arguments of the Oxford Movement.

Bolingbroke, Henry St. John (1678–1751): Henry St. John Bolingbroke, the 1st Lord Viscount, was a prominent English Tory statesman, orator, man of letters, and deist.

Boulanger, André de (1578–1657): André de Boulanger was a French Augustinian monk and preacher, most notable for his burlesque style of preaching marked by his large use of trivial wordplay, witticisms, and jokes.

Bradford, John (1510–1555): John Bradford was an English reformer, royal chaplain to Edward VI, and Protestant martyr. He and John Leaf were condemned to be burned alive as heretics in the reign of Queen "Bloody Mary."

Bray, William "Billy" Trewartha (1794–1868): Billy Bray, as he was commonly called, was a Cornish tin-miner and evangelist. He is described by Spurgeon as an uneducated (albeit, enthusiastic) soul winner.

Brooke, Edward "Squire" (1779–1871): Edward "Squire" Brooke was an English Methodist lay preacher and a contemporary of Charles Spurgeon. He is described by Spurgeon as "just a plain and somewhat quaint preacher of the old, old gospel."

Brummel, George Bryan "Beau" (1778–1840): George Bryan "Beau" Brummel was an English dandy, a gentleman of leisure, and, in a way, a menswear influencer. He is often regarded today as the father of modern menswear.

Bunyan, John (1628–1688): John Bunyan was a celebrated English preacher and author. His classic book, *The Pilgrim's Progress* (1678), is considered by many to be the most characteristic expression of the Puritan religious outlook.

Burgess, Daniel (1645–1713): Daniel Burgess was a popular Reformed and Presbyterian preacher.

Burke, Edmund (1729–1797): Edmund Burke was an Anglo-Irish statesman and political philosopher. He is often seen as laying the foundations of modern conservatism.

Bush, Sargent (1937–2003): Sargent Bush was John Bascom Professor of English at the University of Wisconsin-Madison, and an author.

C

Campbell, Alexander (1788–1866): Alexander Campbell was an Irish-American preacher, philosopher, author, scholar, publisher, orator, and statesman. He was the founder of Bethany College (West Virginia), and cofounder of the Christian Church (Disciples of Christ) in America.

Carlyle, Thomas (1795–1881): Thomas Carlyle was a Scottish historian and essayist. His writings profoundly influenced the culture and art of the Victorian era.

Cartwright, Peter (1785–1872): Peter Cartwright was a pioneering "hellfire and brimstone" Methodist Episcopal preacher and revivalist who was instrumental in America's Second Great Awakening.

Charles I (1600–1649; reigned 1625–1649): Charles I was the eldest surviving son of James VI of Scotland, otherwise known as England's James I (1566–1625; reigned 1567/1603–1625). From his father he acquired a stubborn belief that kings are intended by God to rule. His authoritative rule and quarrels with parliament provoked a civil war that led to his execution.

Charles II (1630–1685; reigned 1660–1685): Charles II was the eldest surviving son of England's executed king, Charles I (1600–1649; reigned 1625–1649). He was eight years old when civil war broke out, and he lived in exile throughout much of the duration of the war and the period of the republican Commonwealth. In 1660 he was invited back to London and restored to his father's throne.

Charlesworth, Vernon J. (1839–1915): Vernon J. Charlesworth was an English Congregational minister, author, and hymnist. He also served as headmaster of Spurgeon's Stockwell Orphanage (1869–1914).

Collingwood, Cuthbert (1748–1810): Cuthbert Collingwood was an admiral in the Royal Navy, and a colleague of Horatio Nelson in several of the British victories of the Napoleonic Wars.

Collyer, William Bengo (1782–1854): William Bengo Collyer was an English Congregational pastor, author, and hymnist. He is said to have preached more sermons than anyone else in his time.

Cook, Valentine (1763–1822): Valentine Cook was an American itinerant Methodist Episcopal minister.

Cranmer, Thomas (1489–1556): Thomas Cranmer was

the first Protestant archbishop of Canterbury (1533–1556). He helped to create the Church of England and wrote many of its official documents, including *The Book of Common Prayer*.

Cromwell, Oliver (1599–1658): Oliver Cromwell was an English soldier and statesman who led parliamentary forces in the English Civil Wars. He governed as lord protector of England, Scotland, and Ireland (reigned 1653–1658) during the republican Commonwealth.

D

Davis, C. A. (flourished mid to late nineteenth century): C. A. Davis was an English Baptist pastor "of Bradford," West Yorkshire, and a writer. Several articles attributed to Davis appeared in Spurgeon's magazine, *The Sword and the Trowel*.

Davis, John (1787–1854): John Davis was an American lawyer, businessman, and politician from Massachusetts. Over a twenty-five-year period, he served in both houses of the U.S. Congress, and for three non-consecutive years as governor of Massachusetts. Because of his reputation for personal integrity, he was known as "Honest John" Davis.

Dawson, William (1773–1841): William Dawson was a "Yorkshire farmer," an English Methodist minister, and a powerful preacher.

Dickens, Charles (1812–1870): Charles Dickens was – and continues to be – the most famous English author of the Victorian era. He penned fifteen novels, five novellas, and countless stories and essays. His best-known works include *Great Expectations, Oliver Twist,* and *A Christmas Carol*.

Donkersley, James (1810–1892): James Donkersley was an English shopkeeper/grocer (according to mid-nineteenth-century Yorkshire censuses). He was also, perhaps, the elder brother to the Wesleyan Methodist minister John Donkersley (1817–1879), and a lay minister himself.

Dow, Lorenzo (1777–1834): Lorenzo Dow was an itinerant American Methodist evangelist, said to have preached to more people than any other preacher of his era. He also became a popular author.

Durham, James (1622–1658): James Durham was a fiery Scottish preacher, known for his intense strength of conviction and seriousness of character.

E

Edward VI (1537–1553; reigned 1547–1553): Edward VI became king of England and Ireland at the age of nine upon the death of his father, Henry VIII. During Edward's reign, the Church of England became more explicitly Protestant – Edward himself was fiercely so. He died at the age of fifteen (presumably from tuberculosis).

Emerson, Ralph Waldo (1803–1882): Ralph Waldo Emerson was an American essayist, poet, and popular philosopher who had begun his career as a Unitarian minister in Boston.

F

Fox, George (1624–1691): George Fox was an English dissenting preacher and missionary. He was a leader in a seventeenth-century Christian awakening from which came the Quaker movement (now known as the Society of Friends or the Friends Church).

G

Gainsborough, Thomas (1727–1788): Thomas Gainsborough was, with Joshua Reynolds (his main rival), the leading portrait painter in England in the later eighteenth century. He was a founding member of the Royal Academy, and he became a favorite painter of King George III and his family.

Garrick, David (1717–1779): David Garrick was a leading actor, playwright, and theatrical producer in eighteenth-century London. From 1747 to 1776, he was a partner in the Drury Lane Theatre.

Gibson, Edmund (1669–1748): Edmund Gibson was an Anglican bishop, prelate, theologian, and author. He is most remembered for his extensive research in ecclesiastical law that resulted in the publication of his monumental *Codex Juris* (1713).

Goodwin, Thomas (1600–1679): Thomas Goodwin, known as "the Elder," was an English theologian and preacher. He served as chaplain to Oliver Cromwell, and was imposed by parliament as president of Magdalen College, Oxford, in 1650.

Gordon, George (1751–1793): George Gordon was an English lord and instigator of the anti-Catholic Gordon riots in London (1780).

Gough, John Bartholomew (1817–1886): John Bartholomew Gough was a reformed drunkard who became an avid and very popular temperance lecturer in the United States and Great Britain.

Grant, James (1802–1879): James Grant was a British author, parliamentary reporter, and newspaper editor. He was a devout Calvinist, and in 1872 he became editor of the *Christian Standard.*

Grimshaw, William (1708–1763): William Grimshaw, a Wesleyan minister, was the outstanding pioneer of the eighteenth-century revival in the north of England. He was a close friend of John Wesley, and reportedly preached the gospel (in and around Haworth) twenty to thirty times a week.

Gruber, Jacob (1778–1850): Jacob Gruber was an American Methodist Episcopal itinerant preacher and pastor.

Guthrie, William (1620–1665): William Guthrie was a Scottish preacher and author, regarded as one of the holiest and ablest of the experimental religious leaders of Scotland.

H

Hall, Robert (1764–1831): Robert Hall was an English Baptist minister, writer, social reformer, and an outstanding preacher.

Hanway, Jonas (d. 1786): Jonas Hanway was the first man to parade an umbrella unashamed in eighteenth-century England, a time and place in which umbrellas were strictly taboo. In the minds of many English people, umbrella usage was symptomatic of a weakness of character, particularly among men; they also regarded umbrellas as too French. Hanway had just purchased his umbrella on a recent trip to France.

Hare, Francis (1671–1740): Francis Hare was an Anglican bishop, theologian, and a very prolific author. Though once a popular preacher, his personality left much to be desired; he was said by one of his contemporaries to have had a "piercing wit" and a "crabby disposition."

Henley, John "Orator" (1692–1756): John "Orator" Henley was a preacher, entrepreneur, and public speaker who for thirty years operated a place of prayer in the heart of London. He was known for his plain arrogance and his flamboyant style of showmanship.

Henry VIII (1491–1547; reigned 1509–1547): Henry VIII was king of England and Ireland, first of the Tudor line. Henry's reign is usually remembered for his six wives, his legendary appetite, and his vindictive temperament; yet many of his regal actions had profound and lasting effects on our modern world – the break with Rome, the Reformation, and the dissolution of the monasteries, to name a few.

Henry, Matthew (1662–1714): Matthew Henry was an English

Nonconformist minister and prolific writer, most famous for his *Commentary on the Whole Bible*. Concerning this celebrated work, Charles Spurgeon remarked, "First among the mighty (commentaries) for general usefulness we are bound to mention the man whose name is a household word, Matthew Henry. He is most pious and pithy, sound and sensible, suggestive and sober, terse and trustworthy."

Hibbard, William "Billy" (1771–1844): William "Billy" Hibbard was a minister in the American Methodist-Episcopalian Church. He is credited with helping to start a number of churches throughout New York, Massachusetts, and Connecticut as a circuit rider.

Hick, Samuel (1758–1829): Samuel Hick was a famous village blacksmith and Methodist lay preacher in Micklefield, Yorkshire (England).

Hill, Rowland (1744–1833): Rowland Hill was the founding pastor of London's Surrey Chapel and a popular evangelist who attracted huge crowds, sometimes up to twenty thousand people, on his preaching tours throughout England. He was an early supporter of the Sunday school movement, and a keen advocate of vaccination against smallpox.

Holliday, Thomas (1797–1858): Thomas Holliday was an English Primitive Methodist pastor. A remark he made to Edward Brooke was instrumental in the young squire's conversion.

Hooper, John (1495–1555): John Hooper was an Anglican bishop, Protestant reformer, and Protestant martyr. Hooper and Archbishop Thomas Cranmer were trusted friends; he helped Cranmer think through the theology of the first *Book of Common Prayer*.

I

Ingalls, Jeremiah (1764–1838): Jeremiah Ingalls was an American composer, hymnist, and church choirmaster. He is remembered primarily for his published compilation of early New England folk hymns, *The Christian Harmony* (1805).

J

Johnson, Samuel (1709-1784): Samuel Johnson was an English critic, biographer, essayist, poet, and lexicographer. His *Dictionary of the English Language* (1755), sometimes published as *Johnson's Dictionary,* is among the most influential dictionaries in the history of the English language.

K

Kempis, Thomas à (1380-1471): Thomas à Kempis was a monastic priest and author of the most popular devotional classic, *The Imitation of Christ* (c. 1418-1427).

L

Lassenius, Johannes (1636-1692): Johannes Lassenius was a German Lutheran theologian, author, and professor at the University of Copenhagen (Copenhagen, Denmark). He was considered one of the most eloquent baroque preachers of his time.

Latimer, Hugh (c. 1487-1555): Hugh Latimer was an English Protestant preacher, royal chaplain, and bishop of Worcester (1535-1539). Arrested during the persecution of Reformers under Queen Mary I, Latimer, along with Nicholas Ridley, was burned at the stake in Oxford, on October 16, 1555.

Laud, William (1573-1645): William Laud was the archbishop of Canterbury and religious advisor to King Charles I.

His persecution of Puritans and other Nonconformists resulted in his trial and execution by the House of Commons.

Lingard, John (1771–1851): John Lingard was an English Roman Catholic priest and historian, the author of *The History and Antiquities of the Anglo-Saxon Church*.

Longfellow, Henry Wadsworth (1807–1881): Henry Wadsworth Longfellow was one of the most widely known and best-loved American poets of the nineteenth century. His original works include the poems "Paul Revere's Ride," "The Song of Hiawatha," and "Evangeline."

Lord, John Holt (no date): John Holt Lord was an English Wesleyan Methodist pastor (Brunswick Chapel House) and author. He wrote a very popular biography on Edward Brooke, titled, *Squire Brooke. A Memorial of Edward Brooke, of Fieldhouse, near Huddersfield, with Extracts from His Diary and Correspondence* (1873).

M

Mann, Horace (1796–1859): Horace Mann was an American educator and the first great American advocate of public education. He believed that, in a democratic society, education should be free and universal, nonsectarian, democratic in method, and reliant on well-trained professional teachers.

Martin, David (no date): David Martin was an American Methodist Episcopal pastor (Fredericktown, Maryland) who published a record of the *Trial of the Rev. Jacob Gruber, Minister in the Methodist Episcopal Church, at the March Term, 1819, in the Frederick County Court, for a Misdemeanor* (1819).

Mary I (1516–1558; reigned 1553–1558): Mary I, also called Mary Tudor, was the first queen to rule England in her own right. She earned the notorious nickname "Bloody Mary" for her persecution of Protestants in a vain attempt to restore Roman Catholicism in England.

Mather, Cotton (1663–1728): Cotton Mather was a New England Puritan minister and author, supporter of the old order of the ruling clergy. American history likes to portray him as the architect and executioner of the Salem Witch Trials.

Middleton, Erasmus (1739–1805): Erasmus Middleton was an Anglican (Calvinist) minister, author, and editor. His most enduring work is the four-volume *Biographia Evangelica, or The Evangelical Biography* (1779–1786).

Milton, John (1608–1674): John Milton, regarded as the greatest English poet – next to Shakespeare – is the author of the language's finest epic poem, "Paradise Lost."

Moody, Dwight L. (1837–1899): Dwight L. Moody was an American evangelist, author, and publisher who founded the Northfield Schools in Massachusetts, Moody Church, and Moody Bible Institute in Chicago. He was connected with the Higher Life movement (otherwise known as Keswickianism).

N

Nelson, Horatio (1758–1805): Horatio Nelson was a British naval commander in the wars with Revolutionary and Napoleonic France. Due to a series of remarkable victories, he is generally regarded as the greatest officer in the history of the Royal Navy.

Nero (37–68): Nero, in his full name of Nero Claudius Caesar Augustus Germanicus, was the fifth Roman emperor (54–68), stepson, and heir of the emperor Claudius. Sensitive and handsome, Nero started out well as emperor, but his early promise gave way to wild extravagance and murder.

Nye, Phillip (1595–1672): Phillip Nye was an English theologian and a dissenting member of the Westminster Assembly of Divines. During the republican Commonwealth, he acted as an advisor to the Lord Protector, Oliver Cromwell, on matters of the church and religion.

O

Osborn, George (1808–1891): George Osborn was an English Wesleyan Methodist minister, author, and scholar. Noted as a powerful speaker, he was twice president of the annual Methodist Conference.

Ouseley, Gideon (1762–1839): Gideon Ouseley was an Irish Methodist preacher, noted as a missionary and rural revivalist.

Owen, John (1616–1683): John Owen was an English pastor, author, chaplain, and adviser to Oliver Cromwell, and the vice-chancellor of Oxford University. He is considered by many to be the greatest of the Puritan theologians.

P

Peters, Hugh (1598–1660): Hugh Peters was a preacher, military advisor, and political propagandist during the English Civil War and the Commonwealth.

Poole, Joshua (1826–1908): Joshua Poole, also known as "Fiddler Joss," was a Yorkshire drunkard, gambler, and wife-beater, who was converted and became a much-respected teetotaler and evangelist.

Pope, Alexander (1688–1744): Alexander Pope was a poet, translator, and satirist of the English Augustan period, best known for his poems "An Essay on Criticism" (1711), "The Rape of the Lock" (1712–1714), "The Dunciad" (1728), and "An Essay on Man" (1733–1734).

Q

N/A (No additional notes).

R

Reynolds, Joshua (1723–1792): Joshua Reynolds was the leading English portraitist of the eighteenth century. When the Royal Academy was founded in 1768, Reynolds was elected its first president, but he was never popular with King George III.

Ridley, Nicholas (c. 1503–1555): Nicholas Ridley was one of the finest academic minds in the early English Reformation. As the appointed bishop of London, he supported the claim of the Protestant Lady Jane Grey to be Edward VI's successor, and thus was arrested upon the accession of Queen Mary I, a Roman Catholic. Nicholas Ridley and Hugh Latimer, both of whom refused to recant, were burned at the stake on October 16, 1555.

Robinson, Robert (1735–1790): Robert Robinson was a Cambridge preacher, scholar, reformer, and Baptist dissenter; in his lifetime a controversial figure, Robinson has remained controversial in the assessments of Baptist historians.

Rogers, George (no date; flourished mid to latter nineteenth century): George Rogers was an English Congregational minister and the first principal of Spurgeon's Pastor's College. A brief biography, as written by Spurgeon for *The Sword and the Trowel* (1866), describes Rogers as one who "has been a Puritan from his childhood, and is a Puritan still."

Ryland, John (1753–1825): John Ryland was an English Baptist minister, writer, and schoolmaster. He was a founder and for ten years the secretary of the Baptist Missionary Society.

S

Sachaverell, Henry (1674–1724): Henry Sachaverell, a popular preacher at Oxford University, was a controversial supporter of the Anglican state whose impeachment by the Whigs enabled the Tories to win control of England's government in 1710.

Sankey, Ira (1840–1908): Ira Sankey was the solo singer/ music director for Dwight L. Moody's evangelistic campaigns in both the United States and Great Britain.

Sherlock, Thomas (1678–1761): Thomas Sherlock was an Anglican bishop, theologian, and author. Church history regards him as a significant contributor to Christian apologetics.

Smith, Sydney (1771–1845): Sydney Smith was one of the foremost English preachers of his day, famous for his wit and charm. He was also a champion of parliamentary reform. Through his writings he perhaps did more than anyone else to change public opinion regarding Roman Catholic emancipation.

South, Robert (1634–1716): Robert South was one of the great Anglican writers and preachers of his age. Although his sermons were marked by homely and humorous appeal, he was known for his vigorous style and quarrelsome temperament; his wit generally leaned towards sarcasm.

Steele, Richard (1672–1729): Richard Steele was an English essayist, dramatist, journalist, and politician, best known as principal author (with Joseph Addison) of the periodicals *The Tatler* and *The Spectator*.

Sterne, Laurence (1713–1768): Laurence Sterne was an Anglican minister and novelist. He is best known for his inventive and humorous work, *The Life and Opinions of Tristram Shandy, Gentleman* (1759).

Stittle, John (1727–1813): John Stittle – converted under the preaching of John Berridge – was an English Calvinist pastor. He was widely regarded as "the Peasant Preacher," and reportedly was able to read, yet could not write.

Swift, Jonathan "Dean" (1667–1745): Jonathan "Dean" Swift was an Anglo-Irish minister, political pamphleteer, satirist, and author; *Gulliver's Travels* (1726) is his most enduring work.

T

Taylor, Edward Thompson (1793–1871): Edward Thompson "Father" Taylor was an uneducated former sailor who became a Methodist minister and served a church for sailors in Boston's North End for forty years.

Taylor, William (1821–1902): William Taylor was an American Methodist Episcopal missionary bishop, mission theorist, and holiness advocate. Spurgeon refers to him as "Father Taylor of California," since he famously preached temperance during California's Gold Rush period (c. 1848–1855).

Thornton, John (1720–1790): John Thornton was a wealthy English merchant and Christian philanthropist. He was once reported to be the richest merchant in England, and the second richest in all of Europe.

Tillotson, John (1630–1694): John Tillotson was an Anglican preacher, scholar, and archbishop of Canterbury (1691–1694).

Timbs, John (1801–1875): John Timbs was an English antiquarian, noted for having assembled and published over 150 compilations in his lifetime.

Trench, Richard Chenevix (1807–1886): Richard Chenevix Trench was an Anglican archbishop, philologist, and poet.

Twain, Mark (1835–1910): Mark Twain – the pen name of Samuel Langhorne Clemens – was a distinguished novelist, fiction writer, essayist, journalist, and literary critic, who ranks among the great figures of American literature. His novel *The Adventures of Huckleberry Finn* (1885) is generally considered his masterpiece.

U

N/A (No additional notes).

V

Venn, Henry (1725–1797): Henry Venn was an evangelical Anglican minister, and founder of a group of social reformers known as the Clapham Sect.

W

Waugh, Alexander (1754–1827): Alexander Waugh was a Scottish Presbyterian minister known for his interdenominational or parachurch ministries. He was a founding member of the London Missionary Society (1795), and was the chairman of the candidate examination committee for the Society for twenty-eight years.

Wesley, John (1703–1791): John Wesley was an Anglican minister, evangelist, and founder – with his brother Charles – of the Methodist movement in the Church of England.

Whitman, Walt (1819–1892): Walt Whitman was an American poet, essayist, and journalist.

Wilks, Matthew (1746–1829): Matthew Wilks was an English evangelical minister. He was one of the fathers of the London Missionary Society, *The Evangelical Magazine,* the Irish Evangelical Society, the Bible Society, and the Religious Tract Society.

Williams, John (1796–1839): John Williams was an English minister and pioneer missionary, active in the South Pacific. He was martyred on the New Hebrides isle of Erromango by native cannibals.

Whitefield, George (1714–1770): George Whitefield was an ordained Anglican priest, itinerant evangelist, and prominent leader of early Methodism, evangelical Protestantism, and the First Great Awakening.

Wright, Ned (b. 1836): Ned Wright was a Bankside thief and ruffian who was converted and became an evangelist. His "thieves' suppers" – raucous gatherings open only to convicted criminals, who were fed on bread and soup before being addressed by the charismatic Wright – were hailed by some in nineteenth-century England as a sort of rough-hewn philanthropy, while others considered his ministry a scam.

X/Y/Z

N/A (No additional notes).

Similar Titles

Words of Warning, by Charles H. Spurgeon

This book, *Words of Warning,* is an analysis of people and the gospel of Christ. Under inspiration of the Holy Spirit, Charles H. Spurgeon sheds light on the many ways people may refuse to come to Christ, but he also shines a brilliant light on how we can be saved. Unsaved or wavering individuals will be convicted, and if they allow it, they will be led to Christ. Sincere Christians will be happy and blessed as they consider the great salvation with which they have been saved.

Available where books are sold.

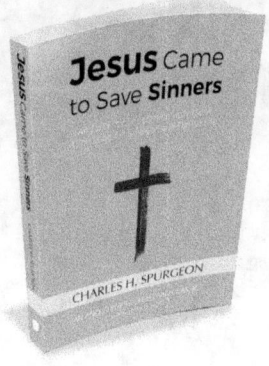

Jesus Came to Save Sinners, by Charles H. Spurgeon

This is a heart-level conversation with you, the reader. Every excuse, reason, and roadblock for not coming to Christ is examined and duly dealt with. If you think you may be too bad, or if perhaps you really are bad and you sin either openly or behind closed doors, you will discover that life in Christ is for you too. You can reject the message of salvation by faith, or you can choose to live a life of sin after professing faith in Christ, but you cannot change the truth as it is, either for yourself or for others. As such, it behooves you and your family to embrace truth, claim it for your own, and be genuinely set free for now and eternity. Come and embrace this free gift of God, and live a victorious life for Him.

Available where books are sold.

According to Promise, by Charles H. Spurgeon

The first part of this book is meant to be a sieve to separate the chaff from the wheat. Use it on your own soul. It may be the most profitable and beneficial work you have ever done. He who looked into his accounts and found that his business was losing money was saved from bankruptcy. This may happen also to you. If, however, you discover that your heavenly business is prospering, it will be a great comfort to you. You cannot lose by honestly searching your own heart.

The second part of this book examines God's promises to His children. The promises of God not only exceed all precedent, but they also exceed all imitation. No one has been able to compete with God in the language of liberality. The promises of God are as much above all other promises as the heavens are above the earth.

Available where books are sold.

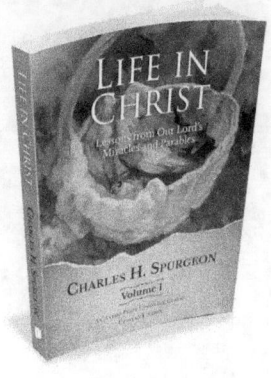

Life in Christ (Vol. 1), by Charles H. Spurgeon

Men who were led by the hand or groped their way along the wall to reach Jesus were touched by his finger and went home without a guide, rejoicing that Jesus Christ had opened their eyes. Jesus is still able to perform such miracles. And, with the power of the Holy Spirit, his Word will be expounded and we'll watch for the signs to follow, expecting to see them at once. Why shouldn't those who read this be blessed with the light of heaven? This is my heart's inmost desire.

I can't put fine words together. I've never studied speech. In fact, my heart loathes the very thought of intentionally speaking with fine words when souls are in danger of eternal separation from God. No, I work to speak straight to your hearts and consciences, and if there is anyone with faith to receive, God will bless them with fresh revelation.

– Charles H. Spurgeon

Available where books are sold.